SNATCHED FROM THE FIRE.

GARY MOORE

DEDICATIONS.

I would like to dedicate this book to several people who have directly touched my life. This has made me richer in every way.

To my Mum, Molly, who passed away in December 2012 leaving a huge hole in my life; who kept me when things were difficult for her and for being the best Mum a man could ever have.

Miss you Mum.

Badly.

To Chris, also now in Glory, for first telling me that I must be born again. Nice one mate!

To my beautiful wife, Jane Poppy Moore, who has encouraged me to write my story and kept me going when the flames were the fiercest. I Love you.

Always have, always will.

Also many thanks to the Norwich YMCA, and especially John Drake, for giving me a room and letting me into a place where I could hear about the one who loved me, Jesus.

But most of all to Jesus, who took me in when I was dirty, lost in sin and hopelessness and gave me a new life in Him. He saw the masterpiece and not the mud.

Yours in His service
Gary Wayne Moore

INTRODUCTION

On Tuesday the 11th January 2011 my life was changed forever.

It was a cold and misty morning as I left work and started up my car, a rather battered old red Skoda Fabia that had been a gift from some very good friends at church, and began the very familiar 45 minute journey back to Canterbury, Kent. It had been a very long and extremely busy night in my job as an Emergency Medical Advisor for the South East Kent ambulance service taking 999 calls from the public. I had worked almost without a break for a full 12 hour shift. But it was a job I really enjoyed so it was not a burden to me and I really enjoyed the challenge, which was just as well as it was perhaps the most demanding job I had ever had. We were the tip of the sword dealing with terrible emergencies even before the ambulance crews arrived on scene to take over. Very often what happened on the initial call to us in the Emergency Call Centre made the difference between life and death as we triaged the patient over the telephone.

I wound down the window and enjoyed the chilled morning air flowing over my face and turned my I-pod on to one of my favorite songs, a track by Third Day, called Follow Me. I turned out of the car park under the automatic barrier and headed along Heath road planning to reach the A20 Ashford road that would take me home, looking forwards to a good sleep.

Unfortunately I never made it home.

Although I was fatigued I wasn't too concerned about driving in a tired condition. For many years I had been a black cab taxi driver and was used to long hours and late nights and early mornings, pushing through the tiredness barrier, building up a kind of stamina against exhaustion.

At this time of the morning there was little traffic on the back roads and I enjoyed the emptiness and freedom, using both sides of the road in a safe manner. I passed Leeds castle, just on the outskirts of Maidstone, Kent and settled down for the familiar journey along the A20 my mind already in that particular kind of autopilot that driving the same route brings.

As I approached a bend in the road I simply fell asleep and my car hurtled off the tarmac, over a grass verge, down a slope and smashed headlong into some very solid trees at approximately fifty to sixty miles per hour. The car crumpled around me on impact, sounding like the very crack of doom itself, a cacophony of appalling noise and action. Then there was that particular silences as if the very air was stunned by the atrocity of the accident and nature couldn't look on.

As the car didn't have an airbag my chest took the full impact as I was crushed up against the steering wheel, breaking most of my ribs and causing a potential deadly injury, left chest flail. My left arm was also smashed and broken in several places, bones sticking out through the skin. I broke my collar bone and also a bone in my thoracic spine, T4, along with a whole host of cuts and bruises to my legs. I was like an egg dropped from height, broken and smashed by the impact, my life just as fragile and so easily lost.

The first few seconds after the impact were terrifying as such dreadful pain like I had never known before ripped me apart and I was struggling to catch every breath, stunned by what had so suddenly happened. One moment I had been driving, the next I was fighting for my very life, trying to make sense of what had just happened, so swiftly had events unfolded. I was very badly disorientated yet somehow was also acutely aware of the appalling peril I was now in. Death itself was hovering over the roof of the car, like some awful vulture waiting for carrion.

I remember screaming in sheer terror and agony; then trying frenziedly to get out of the car door. But there wasn't a chance of that as the car had crumpled very badly, body work twisting and jamming the driver's door solid. There was no way I could have opened the door anyway as it was up tight against a tree. I hammered fruitlessly on the glass window with my right hand and elbow. I then tried to reach to my left side and undo my safety belt but found I couldn't move. Besides my left arm was very badly broken in several places bones sticking out through the skin and was useless and just to move it was agony. I was trapped, pinned against the steering wheel, as helpless as I could possibly be. An awful feeling of impending doom suddenly gripped me, like feeling a bridge tremble underfoot when suspended over a deep chasm.

Things were about to get considerably worse.

There was a sudden overwhelming smell of petrol; then a wisp of smoke caught my eye from the front of the car and then to my horror Yellow flames suddenly curled around the raised and crumpled bonnet. A huge wave of terror hit me with tsunami like force as I realized that I was about to burn to death, trapped inside the car. I stared at the bonnet for several seconds as the red paint began to bubble and blister in the heat, as if the car was being eaten alive by the fire, and I was hardly able to register what I was seeing so great was the shock. The truth soon thrust home as sharp as a cold blade. I was going to die in the fire.

I thrashed around trying to get out, to wriggle loose, to get as far away as possible from those dreadful, hungry flames, but my appalling injuries and the damage to the car made it impossible to move. Yet, somehow, I managed to get the safety belt undone, the agony of twisting indescribable but I was prepared to do anything, to undergo any amount of pain to escape a certain gruesome death. I stared at the flames, screaming in sheer terror. I cried out in desperation, *"God, don't let me burn alive!"*

For what seemed like several long minutes I sat there, crying out, praying, screaming in pain and most of all, in absolute stark fear, as those terrible flames grew bolder and closer with each passing second. The heat built up inside the car until it was like standing near a roaring bonfire on a cold November's night but impossible to pull away.

Then, suddenly, I heard muted voices outside above the roar of the flames, shouting and full of urgency, and I yelled out to them in case they had not seen me, didn't realize that there was someone alive inside the burning wreck. Hope leaped inside of me like a living thing and I screamed out for help. Then the passenger door was violently wrenched open and a wave of cool fresh air pushed back the heat from the inferno for a second, then surged back in again as if unwilling to let me go. The flames were by now inside the passenger foot well by my feet in the car. Hungry flames leapt from the dashboard melting the plastic trim, only inches away from my face. It was a desperate situation and I knew I was just seconds away from being burnt to death, the worst fate I could imagine. An absolute nightmare way to die.

The next few minutes were a blur of terror and torment as I was dragged out across the passenger seat and onto the damp grass of the slope. The agony at being pulled out was enough to cause me to lose consciousness for a few moments but I can vividly remember watching my feet leaving the car, and the grunts and shouts of my rescuers as they risked all to help me as they pulled me out of what was certainly my funeral pyre.

God had heard my cry for help and intervened in the shape of a retired fireman, Ian Ridges. He had heard the crash and rushed over to help. Two other passing motorists had also stopped and helped him rescue me as he led the way.

They had saved me from almost certain death but it was God who had had the last say in the matter. It wasn't my day to die. It was a case of thus far and no further.

As I lay there on the dew covered grass, writhing in agony, fighting for my very life, I watched in horror as the flames took hold of the car and then whooshed through consuming the whole of the interior, the very place I had just been sitting. Much later on I was told that it had only been 20 seconds from the time I was pulled from the car to the car being engulfed in flames.

20 seconds between burning to death and living. Not long.

As I lay there on the damp ground the full impact of what had happened hit home, as did the pain. Everything started to go dark and I knew that I was dying, there and then, and a pit of bottomless fear began to pull me down, like water rushing down a hole and as inexorable.

Ian had pulled me about ten feet away from the burning car, and both our clothes were smoldering with the radiated heat from the fire. It wasn't possible to move me any further away as my injuries were appalling. I lay there, my head cradled on Ian's knees, struggling to live. The crackling, hissing, as the car was consumed by fire is still ringing in my ears to this very day and I still frequently smell smoke, even indoors.

There and then I made a choice and I managed to begin to speak out, to declare, "I choose to live. I am not going to die "I kept repeating these words over and over, forcing myself to stay awake. I didn't dare close my eyes for fear that if I did then it would all be over and I would slip away into the dark and die, as if some unseen hand was waiting to drag me away into death.

Vivid color images of those I dearly loved flashed through my mind and I wondered if this is what happened when you died and had your life rushing before your eyes. At the forefront of this kaleidoscope of sights and sounds were Jane, then my fiancée and now my beloved wife. We were due to marry in just a few weeks and there was no way was I going to let her down; pictures of my two sons and grandchildren, laughing and smiling all followed. All that I loved and held dear passed before my eyes and I decided that I had to live for them and I was suddenly filled with an incredible resolve to stay alive.

I was not going to die and that was that!

The pain in my left arm was terrible and could feel the bone grate if I moved but the agony from my chest injuries was far worse and I knew that I was in deep, deep trouble. I didn't know then just how seriously injured I actually was. The battle to survive had only just started. Over the next few weeks in intensive care I brushed with death a further four times and narrowly escaped each time.

I remember the Fire Brigade and Ambulance crews arriving on scene and very soon the whole place was filled people whose sole aim was to help me survive. One of the firemen called over to the paramedics who had just begun to triage me to see what my injuries were, telling them in no uncertain terms to move me well back from the burning car as they were worried that it was going to explode. I knew that the car had a full tank of petrol.

I will never forget what happened next.

The two paramedics looked at each other and moved around until they had placed their own bodies between me and the flaming vehicle, to protect me. It was yet another act of unselfish bravery and kindness that terrible morning putting them in danger to help me. Even though I worked for the emergency services I am still amazed at bravery. What was even more amazing was that Ian never moved away, kneeling and supporting my head to keep my airway open to help me breathe.

A short time later I heard an incredibly loud crump as the fuel tank ignited and the percussion washed over us, but not a single person was injured. Another act of God's grace that morning.

Minutes later I was maneuvered onto a stretcher, then into the back of the ambulance, ready for the high speed dash to hospital, and the battle of all battles just to keep alive.

As the ambulance pulled away, blue lights flashing and siren wailing, I thought back to the way I met the God who had delivered me from the fiery furnace and from burning alive, struggling and fighting to stay alive.

CHAPTER ONE.

Life began for me in very humble surroundings. I was born in 1961 in the university town of Cambridge, England. My mother, Molly Moore, was according to my birth certificate, a scientific instrument assembler who worked in a local factory.

My mum was a single parent, choosing to bring me up alone, without the aid or help of my father. Some stories are best left untold.

I have never delved too much into this early time. All I know for sure is that there was trouble at home with my Granddad and my mum had to leave home before I was born.

Simple as that.

I know that the early years were very tough for my mum and looking back now, I only have the greatest regard and respect for her on how she took life full on and didn't flinch, doing her best for me against all the odds. Even when it was suggested to her that she had me aborted, she didn't listen, leaving home rather than have me killed. What an incredible mum to go to such lengths to save me! It seems that I was having narrow escapes even before I was born.

Some of my earliest childhood memories are of run down rooms or damp and dingy flats, and as I grew up there were one or two places that really stuck in my mind as being particularly awful. The slums down Old Palace road were such a place. They had been condemned to be torn down but single parent families were still placed there by Norwich City Council right up until the day they were demolished. Huge wooden railway sleepers were outside the front, propped up against the walls, to keep the house from falling down, and were the only things holding it up. They always frightened me and looked dangerous.

The one stable point in my early life was my Granny and Granddad Moore, who lived in the small Suffolk market town of Beccles, about twenty miles from Lowestoft on the east coast.

23 Common Lane was a safe and secure place for me, not only then but right up until later in life when things were really bad for me. Granny's house was always a bolt hole and a refuge. A safe place for me to go to in times of trouble.

Whenever I think of my Granddad, Ernie Moore, I have a mental picture of him in an old check shirt, leaning on a spade in the back garden, rolling a cigarette. He cherished his garden and spent hours there digging, planting and tending his vegetables. Everything from potatoes to green beans was grown in the garden and I used to help when I stayed there. He also loved to roll his own cigarettes and he used a green Old Holborn tin to keep his tobacco and papers in. I loved to watch him as he rolled and then smoked them, often leaning on his spade, just enjoying the moment of contentment, smoke curling away on the breeze. I used to wonder what he was thinking about. I just enjoyed those moments and felt a deep contentment never experienced anywhere else.

There was one dark cold November's night that I can remember as though it was yesterday. We had a great big bonfire, right at the very bottom of the garden. We had spent several days building it up, dumping all the old garden rubbish on it, in fact everything I could find. A railway track was at the very end of the garden just over a hedge, with several trains a day thundering past. I always jumped and waved as they sped past and was often rewarded with a wave from some passenger looking out of the train window. It always made my day when that happened.

The night was very cold and very clear with a slight frost about it and it seemed as though every star in the heavens were out on display just for me to see and enjoy. The smoke from the bonfire billowed up into the night sky and the myriad of tiny sparks floating up and away into the night sky on the heat of the fire fascinated me. I shone my torch beam through the smoke, really impressed at the sight, caught up in a Star Wars fantasy of using a light sabre, as I cut and sliced my way through untold number of alien invaders!

It was brilliant as I danced around the fire, heat on my face as I jumped around. I was just enjoying being with my Granddad, simply being a small boy without a care in the world for that night. Like all small boys should. Innocence and happiness for a short, uninterrupted space of time. Very rare in this sad untidy world we live in.

Granddad explained that my light beam, reaching up and into the smoky night sky wouldn't reach the stars for hundreds, if not thousands, of years yet. A simple, yet clear explanation of the speed of light.

" You never know, Gary, there could be some little Martian boy standing outside with his Martian Granddad looking up at the stars one night and suddenly see a twinkle of light from planet earth." he said as we stood there, his hand on my shoulder, looking up with me. "And maybe if we were here in thousands of years' time, we could get his reply."

Needless to say I was captured by the thought of it all and spent the time before I was taken in to bed sending messages to Mars, my imagination bright and fuelled. I didn't have a great deal of sleep that night as I shined the torch light out of my bedroom window until I literally fell asleep on the window ledge, my torch batteries dim and spent.

I can also vividly remember playing darts with my Granddad, hour after hour, throwing the darts at the dartboard nailed up on the shed door. I was pretty good at one stage, and was able to hit whatever number on the board I threw at. I was never as good as Granddad, though. He was great. It seems to me now that I was always staying there, coming over by bus the 20 miles from Norwich to Beccles, always travelling alone, with Gran meeting me at the small brick built bus stop. I was a handful at home but with Gran and Granddad I was as good as gold.

Once we had these simple plastic and elastic band pop guns and handfuls of dried peas, which we fired at everything and anything that moved in the garden. One day Granddad and me made a castle out of old yoghurt pots and cleaned out baked bean tins and then we built and destroyed it many times. Happy times, just like any little boy should have.

But as much as I loved my Granddad, it was Granny I loved with all my heart. She was the center of my young life.

All through my life, right up until the time she died, she always took great pleasure in making me know that I was her favorite grandchild. I was her special one, no matter what I had done, or more to the point what I hadn't done. No judging me even when I went off the rails. To Gran, I was just Gary, her favorite Grandson.

And that was enough for me. Unconditional love is all a child needs.

There was one infamous occasion when I ran away from home. I was eight or nine years old and really hated school and home. So one day, it was very sunny I remember, I ran away from Norwich and walked the 24 miles to get to Granny and Granddad's. No mean task for a boy of my age wearing thin worn shoes.

It took me at least 12 hours in the heat, but I pushed on and on, following the road signs, heading for the safety of Gran's. I was so thirsty at one stage that I drank from a puddle by the side of the road. I think that I had seen someone do it in a war film. Good enough for me.

When I finally got to Beccles, exhausted and hungry, I pressed the doorbell and waited. I was nearly asleep on my feet, I was that deadbeat. When Granny answered, looking more than a little surprised, I just burst into a flood of tears. I was worn out and my feet were a sea of blisters and swollen very badly and bleeding. I had hobbled the last few miles on willpower alone, the thin cheap shoes soon falling apart. Gran welcomed me in with hugs and kisses and set me in the front room with Granddad who looked just as surprised to see me. He simply patted the space next to him on the sofa and I sat down with him, safe and sound at last. No explanation needed. I cried and cried.

I told them that I had run away and wanted to stay with them. Gran just smiled and made me a cup of her tea, followed by something to eat, a cheese sandwich with mustard.

Later that night as I lay tucked up in bed, washed and fed and greatly relieved, I heard the doorbell ringing and I looked out the window. It was the police! I crept back into bed and pretended to be asleep, pulling the blankets up and over my head. There was no way I was going back to Norwich! I decided there and then that if they wanted to take me back that night then I would rather walk another 20 miles right now! I would've done it as well, I know that for sure.

I heard Granny talking in low tones with the policeman and that, yes; I was fine if not very sore and blistered. It had never occurred to me that my mum would be worried and upset as to where I had gone and it wasn't until I heard them talking that it entered my head. To this day I cannot remember exactly why I ran away that Time. Things were hard at home and I realize now that I wasn't a lot of help to my Mum and probably never was.

Granny came up and told me what had happened. The policeman was going to let my mum know I was all right and in Beccles, safe and secure. In all my life I don't think that I had felt as relieved as I did that night lying there in bed, knowing I could stay with Gran.

As I lay there, after Gran had gone, I looked down under the bedclothes at my feet, aching as they were, and "Well done feet. You got me here!" I was soon fast asleep, shattered as I was.

My bedroom I used whenever I stayed at my Grans was a small box room at the back of the house looking out onto the rear garden. The wallpaper had pictures of clowns and trains. It was small but I knew that it was always mine when I stayed. There was a landing leading to the bathroom with the stairs on the left. Gran used to leave the light on for me, the door slightly ajar. Sometimes she would even let me have a special night light candle in the winter months.

Every night at about 10pm I used to sit up and stare out of the curtains towards the bottom of the garden where the train track cut through the trees, and wait for the train that ran from Lowestoft to Ipswich to come past. Yellow carriage lights and the clacking of the wheels on the track used to send a shiver down my spine with excitement. I always yearned to know who was on the train, where they were going to, what they were planning to do. I was always without exception lost in a world of thought after the train had rattled by in a few swift seconds. I promised myself that one day I would take a long, long journey by train, maybe even to the very ends of the world.

Little did I know that many years later that I would have a journey of a lifetime when I travelled on the Trans-Siberian Express, long days and nights, rumbling across central Siberia.

CHAPTER TWO

In all of my early years the closest I came to having anything to do, even vaguely, with religion was watching the marching band of the Salvation Army. On Sunday mornings, and it always seemed very early, I would awaken to hear the deep bass drum beat as the Sally Army band marched along Common Lane in Beccles heading for the large green grass area just across from the house. I can still recall that deep booming of the drum heralding the arrival of the band.

It was a sight that always (even now) sent a shiver of excitement down my spine. I always felt, for reasons unknown to me, happy and full of joy at the sight of the men and woman, resplendent in their uniforms, marching in step to the beat of the bass drum, so smart and full of purpose; Gods very own brass band.

The red ribbons in the black bonnets of the ladies struck me as brilliant, so vibrant but even now I cannot adequately describe how I felt at the sight. Almost as though I should have been a part of them.

Then there would be a pause in things as they assembled and arranged themselves on the green, getting their music ready, watching the bandmaster. By this time there would be many others from the street looking out of their windows or even walking outside to stand nearby to enjoy what was to come.

Then the bandmaster would say something that I could never quite hear and then the band would begin to play. A thrill of pleasure would wash over me and I would suddenly feel so alive, wanting to rush outside in my pajamas and join in with them! It
't until years later that I found out what they stood for. For their passionate love for the lost and hurting in this sad and untidy world that we live in, being there for many people even when everyone else has given up on them and didn't give a damn any longer for their needs as human beings. The Salvation Army goes into places where even Angels fear to tread at times.

Saturday mornings were great at Grans. It was baking day!

My Granny made meat pies like no one else could do and they had a taste all of their own, never to be repeated by any I have ever tried. Along with her cheese straws and various cakes it was a treasure trove to me. I would help her out at the kitchen table, hoping, waiting, for the chance to lick out the mixing bowls with their wonderful contents. The smell of the pies and cheese straws as they baked would almost make my mouth water in anticipation of the moment they were to come out of the oven and I could get stuck in!

Also Granny had REAL butter!

Sometimes in the winter when it was very cold I would have the task of getting the butter out of the larder and setting it down near to the open coal fire so that the butter would soften, making it easier to spread. I always managed to get sticky fingers before my tea!

Happy, happy times.

Life back home was pretty tough and on top of this I was having a hard time at school. Because of my size, quite large, I had a habit of getting into fights and scrapes, even when they were nothing to do with me. I had a reputation as a fighter and a bully at times. I was good with my fists and feet. I had to be.

There were, however, great moments of joy, such as the time I won a huge cake in a school raffle. It was the biggest cake I had ever seen in my life. I don't know if I have seen one that size since. It was too big for me to carry home and since I could never hope to get it home by myself, a teacher with her car volunteered to give me a lift. I felt hugely important driving home with the cake on the backseat. Money was always scarce and this would be a welcome treat for us all.

Mum and Deborah, my younger sister, were amazed as I proudly walked, or should I say staggered in, struggling to not bend under the weight of the cake. "Look what I've won!" There was joy in the house that day. I felt proud and laughed and laughed at the expressions on my mum's faces at the sight of the cake.

The cake was great and lasted quite a while.

Over the years mum had relationships with a few American servicemen. They were good men who took care of mum and us for the most part. But long-term concrete relationships were never to be. At the time I just accepted things as normal, never understanding or imagining just how these events were forming my character, and this would affect me in later life.

The more I was hurt and touched by these broken relationships the more I turned to my own company, until I reached a point when I was more comfortable just being on my own. I was being molded into a loner, but not by choice. I just found that when alone no one could hurt me or get at me. This followed me through my entire life.

In time I had a younger brother, Darren. He was good kid and I loved him dearly. One Memory that sticks out was the time that we lost him in the snow!

My sister, Debbie, and I had been outside playing in the deep snow that had fallen. She was 5 and I was about 8. Darren was about six month old. We had taken him outside with us, bundled up in a warm snowsuit. We had fun as we rolled him in the snow and built a snowman, complete with a carrot for a nose. Then mum called us in for tea and we both ran inside, cold and ready for something warm to eat, pulling off our wet, and snow covered coats.

Halfway through tea mum asked where Darren was. We realized to our horror that we had forgotten to bring him in with us! We rushed out, but couldn't find him for what seemed like ages. Wrapped up as he was, he had fallen fast asleep in the snow where I had thrown him! It took us about 20 minutes to discover where he was! We laugh about it now but it had been serious then.

Another move loomed up on us and we left Norwich and headed out to a new town, Thetford.

Thetford was a purpose built town to house the London overspill, even though London was over 100 miles away. Various factories had been built to provide employment to cater for the influx of people, moving to what had been optimistically called a 'better life away from the big city'. What had once been a small market town was now a sprawling complex of houses and schools and new roads. And with it the crime that always followed. I soon got involved with older lads who had a history of crime.

The housing estate we lived on was called St Martins way and was a bit like a rabbit warren of narrow alleyways that twisted and turned and was full of close packed houses. I could never understand why the houses were built so close together when there was so much land surrounding the town.

There was, however, one saving grace to the place and that was that we were surrounded on three sides by Thetford Forest, run and managed by the Forestry Commission. Mile after square mile of untouched forest, mainly tall pine. After a while the woodland became my second home as I explored my new world, alone and enjoying it.

During our first summer there before school began, I started to explore, by myself of course, the massive expanse of forest. At first I kept close to the edges within earshot of the A11 road that ran to one side. I could hear the vehicles driving past and so had a point of reference to head to if I got lost. It was a bit like a learner sailor keeping in sight of land. But my confidence grew that I could make it out as I began to recognize where I was, I moved further and further into the wooded depths of the forest. It was great. I was in my element and alone. I often went for days without speaking to a single other human being.

The sheer silence of the woods was unnerving to me at first and really quite scary. But it soon became a place of confidence and familiarity, as I grew used to the various tracks that crisscrossed the forest, where the forestry workers moved about, carrying the trees they cut down. I also placed my own markers around the place, sometimes leaving a bottle of water here and there just in case I ran short. I also dug small holes where I placed tins of beans and tinned sausages and waterproofed matches and various, useful objects I may have needed in an emergency.

I loved the sounds of the birds and the sudden urgent scurrying of small animals, many times unseen. Then there was the deer that wandered about, safe from danger. I loved nothing more than to lie up and watch as deer foraged and frolicked, unaware that anyone was watching them. It was a place of solitude and I loved it.

Many times I made simple lean-tos and hides to rest in and sometime even to sleep in as well. Again I would stock these places with water and tins of beans and waterproof matches to make a fire if needed. Often I would make a small fire and place potatoes in the embers to bake them. Real tasty. I felt I was the master of my environment, Emperor of my own little Kingdom.

As I roamed the woods, sometime up to 14 hours a day, I would quite often pretend that I was a Special Forces soldier tracking down some dangerous enemy that only I could find and take out. On occasion, when other people were out walking in the forest, I would silently track them as well, moving from tree to tree, never more than a few meters away from them. There was one time when a forest warden chased me, since much of the land was private and no one was really allowed on. I soon lost him. But that didn't bother me. One reason for keeping people out was that there was an Army firing range in the middle of the forest and there was real danger of walking into it. There were notices posted around warning people that if the red flags were flying you had better keep well away. But you couldn't take a chance, not with live ammunition being fired, so there were strict penalties for being caught in the Forest.

Several times when the Army was firing live rounds on the long sandy range, there I was hidden just yards away from them, watching and waiting to see if they left anything behind that I could steal. It was a real buzz to me to be that close and not be seen. I would have been in deep trouble if I had been caught! Once I was only yards away from the actual targets that were being fired at, hidden behind the sandbank. Incredibly dangerous to say the least but that was the way I was at age fourteen.

As the summer closed I began a new school, Staniforth Secondary Modern. And right from the start I was in trouble again because of my size. Fighting, swearing and disruptive behavior in class had me being a regular visitor to the headmaster, Mr. Briggs. Try as I might, I could never seem to avoid trouble. Not that I tried too hard! There was a certain buzz at being in trouble. It made me feel good!

The one saving grace for me at school, however, was the game of rugby.

My math's teacher was a giant of a man called Mr. Hathaway. He was a nice even-tempered sort of person who had the task of teaching the lower end of pupils the basics of mathematics. No easy assignment for anyone. But he managed it to some degree. It was nice to have a teacher who seemed to understand what we couldn't and communicate it to us. His huge size also kept the class in check. Even me. He was a giant of a man. He was also a Christian, something I found out years later.

Mr. Hathaway taught the Rugby lessons and that was what gained him respect for many of us lads, especially me. He was huge, with a capital H. On the field he made us work hard but it was enjoyable. Once I nearly killed myself as I tackled him head on, not something that you really wanted to do. I hit him head on and stopped like I had hit a brick wall. My teeth rattled in my head but I wasn't one to back off. I reasoned that if I could take him down, anyone else would be a pushover. Take out the biggest first.

After this much talked about event I was nicknamed "The Tank." It did wonders for my reputation as a hard lad. What no one knew was that I would never try to tackle him again!

School life was tough for me and it seemed no matter how hard I tried I could never do well. My home life was having a bad effect on me. My whole attitude was appalling and even now, years later, I feel ashamed at how I was then.

Mum had met and taken a real liking to an American serviceman called Bob Schlomann and things were looking very serious to me. I had this awful felling that if mum took him seriously and they got married, as I had heard was in the air from an overheard conversation, then I was going to have to buckle down. And that, as far as I was concerned, would never do at all. My behavior over the years had been atrocious most of the time. I blamed mum for everything.

I could see trouble looming for me if they married. So I set out to make things as hard for Bob as I could. So I played up and gave it the big one.

I swore about the house as much as I could. I stole from Bob and mum whenever I could. If it wasn't nailed down it went missing. I stayed out late then woke everyone up when I got back late banging on the door. I ignored Bob as much as I could even when he spoke to me. I did all I could to cause disruption in the house. Week after week I was intent on driving that man out of my life. My entire lifestyle was designed to upset and intimidate him.

In a nutshell I made life a living hell for my family. And it didn't bother me one little bit. Not in the slightest. I wanted things my own way, no matter what it took.

Looking back I can see just how hard it must have been for Bob. He was taking on a ready-made family with two sons and a daughter already in place. Years later I found myself in the same position. I soon realized that it takes real guts for any man to do that. He must have really loved my mum. But I never saw that. Just what I wanted and that was that as far as I was concerned.

Events came to a head when I attacked mum with a large carving knife. It took place in the kitchen. By the grace of God she wasn't hurt, just very badly frightened. I can still see that moment in time as though it happened five minutes ago. It seemed that day as though everything in my life had simply boiled over in me and a river of molten rage and anger erupted out of me. All the years of hurts and frustrations that had been just below the surface came bursting out in a storm of anger and violence directed against my mum. To this day neither of us can remember what triggered me off. In fact we have never talked about it since that time.

The sheer pain of being fatherless, the hopelessness I had felt so many times when we had next to nothing, the anger at always feeling different from everyone else. The hurt of seeing others who had what I didn't' have. Of having to go to school many times with holes in my shoes. Of having to wear older clothes when others at school wore new. The anguish at having friends who had Dads who loved them. The very thing I longed for but could never have. It was all so unfair. And it hurt. And so I lashed out.

I left the house quickly, throwing the knife away as I went, cursing and swearing at anyone I met. I slept rough that night not wanting to go anywhere near home. I wasn't worried about what Bob would do. I was tough and the mood I was in I would have gladly used the knife on him. Knives were to feature in my life whenever I was in trouble, death coming very close on several occasions' later on in life.

I knew deep down that I was out of order but I didn't care. But as the long cold night wore on I began to have my doubts about what I had done. All I had ever wanted in my life was to be loved and cared for. Same as everyone else. I will never know what I would have done if it hadn't been for Granny and Granddad. For the normality they gave me. Just loving me, as I was, not for what I wasn't or couldn't possibly be.

I decided early in the morning to go home and to face up to what I had done. I promised myself that I would even try to apologize to her for what I had said and done. Maybe it would be possible to sort out a few things. Who knows?

As I walked in through the back gate I was still pondering how I could get back home, with the minimum of groveling to mum, trying to find some words to express it all. The sight that met me stopped me dead in my tracks.

All of my clothes were out in the back garden on the grass, scattered about like they had been thrown out of my bedroom window. Shirts, trousers, shorts, pants and socks, just laying there on the grass. It was immediately obvious to me that they had been laid out there all night, as everything was damp.

I wondered what the hell had happened. Had there been a fire, or a burglary. What?

The back door was locked as I tried to open it. I could see Mum and Bob through the glass window. I knocked on the glass.

"What's going on?" I asked. Bob stood at the door and spoke through, not even opening it. "You're out of here. You are not welcome in this house after what you have done."

I was stunned! They couldn't do this to me. I was only fifteen years old. How could they put me out? For once in my life I was speechless!

Then the realization struck me that this was for real. It hit me hard in that moment that what I had done was now catching me up, big time. I was out and there was no way I was going to get back inside the house. I'd blown it. For once there was no fight in me. It had happened too quickly to respond as I normally would have done with confident, abusive words and gestures.

I slowly gathered up my belongings, stuffing them into my sleeping bag, unable to take in what was happening to me. I remember seeing Debbie at her bedroom window. She looked shocked. I looked up at her for some sign of support but got none, as I hadn't been too nice to her. Once I had even shot her on purpose with my powerful air-pistol. That had hurt her badly and she hadn't forgotten that. Didn't blame her really.

The sleeping bag full, I slung it over my shoulder, like some surreal Father Christmas, and walked away, very close to tears, too stunned to think about what I would do next.

There have been a few memorable low points in my life. This time sticks out as one of them, but not the worst by far. The only other time I had felt this hopeless up to this point in my life was when mum had been taken very badly ill with yellow jaundice when I was about 9 years old. Debbie and I had been placed in children's home very quickly. It was Christmas time, just a few days before in fact, and I remember how the other kids who lived there had all been invited to a special party for them the day after we both arrived. But not Debbie and me. We were left almost alone in the home. To this day I cannot understand why they couldn't have allowed two other kids to go along and join in.

When they all came back, full of happiness and loaded down with presents, I had just sat with Debbie and looked on. It was a bad time for both of us. No one seemed to care about the two of us. To this day I have trouble enjoying Christmas.

It was a bad Christmas that year for all of us. I don't know why we were never taken to Grans. It wasn't until years later that Gran told me that she'd never been told until it was too late to do anything.

It was a Sunday morning when I was thrown out of home and so it was quiet everywhere. As I walked along I could smell that unmistakable aroma of Sunday roast dinners being prepared, getting ready to be served up. It made things worse to know that I wouldn't be having one that day. I had no idea where to go so I hid my sleeping bag behind the courthouse by Button Island in the center of Thetford shopping precinct. I had to climb over an iron railing to get there so I reasoned they would be safe.

I had a sudden need to talk to someone, anyone, at that point. But I had no real mates and my girlfriend was away on holiday. I felt rather lonely, even for me.

For some reason I decided to call the Samaritans. I had seen a program about the Samaritans on the telly and it seemed a good idea to speak to them. I checked their address in the phone book and decided there and then to go to Bury St Edmunds, some twelve miles away, where their local office was, and see someone. I felt I would like to talk to someone face to face rather than down a telephone line.

I had to hitch hike the 12 miles, but I knew it would give me time to think about what I would say when I arrived. I wasn't any good at talking to people about my feelings and certainly not at times like this.

The lady who met me at the Samaritans office was very kind and made me a nice cup of tea when I finally made it there. She looked as though she understood my many problems as I poured out my heart to her. I'd never opened myself up to anyone like this before in my life. It felt good to get it all out. There were a few tears as well, something I had never done before in front of anyone, let alone a perfect stranger.

As I talked, she chipped in occasionally with some really good advice and after a while I calmed down, feeling better for it all. But there was still the problem of where I could go. My head was getting sorted out but now my body needed it as well. I was homeless and night was closing in fast.

After explaining, yet again, why I couldn't go home, I felt as though I had hit a brick wall. As good as it was to talk, what I needed now was practical help. And fast.

The lady, as good as she was at listening to me, couldn't help me at all. The only option, she said, was to get the social services involved since I was so young. And that was a big NO as far as I was concerned. I'd had one brush with them, and that was enough for me. I decided that I would sort things out myself, quite how I had no idea whatsoever.

So after thanking her politely for her time and help, I hitched back to Thetford, looking forward to another night sleeping out rough.

As I lay in my sleeping bag that night, huddled against the cold, the full understanding of what I had done sunk in. I knew that I was trouble most of the time, but what could I do about it?

There was a huge bubble of bitterness inside of me that was causing so much hurt to me and then spilling out to touch and hurt all those around me, but I had no idea how to find the peace of mind and spirit that I so desperately needed in my life. This terrible cancer of bitterness at life was to be the cause of my drinking problems later on in life. It was eating me away from the inside, unseen except for the anger that surfaced on occasion, molten hot and terribly dangerous to anyone nearby.

I just knew that one way or another all the trouble in life was my fault. Somehow, I don't know why, I even blamed myself for the fact that I didn't have a Dad. As if I could of done anything about the situation! Not for the first time that night I considered suicide. That was how I honestly felt. 15 years old and already so tired with life and what it had to offer that I wanted to end it. I wonder how many others Gary's there are out there right now, just the same as I was, desperate and lonely. They need to be touched with the love of Jesus. All I had ever wanted was to be loved. I may as well of have tried to fly to the moon. Love and peace seemed that far away and just as impossible to attain.

Early in the morning of that long cold night, I thought about heading over to Gran's. I could just picture my small box room and that comfortable warm bed, but I knew that she would be worried about me being kicked out. I stayed put, not wanting any of my problems to hurt her.

Next day I managed to stay with a friend for a while, sleeping on the couch. Eventually I was allowed back home.

Not long after my return home I found myself short of cash. My pocket money wasn't enough for me to get by on. A mate told me that there was a paper round going down at the newsagents. I laughed as I remembered what had happened the last time I'd been delivering newspapers. I'd ended up at court! Those in my school year still talked about the Great Sport Shop Robbery! It was quite an event!

CHAPTER THREE.

I was aged 14 and up to no good on a regular basis. Several of the lads I hung about with had early morning newspaper delivery jobs. Up at 5am five days a week in all weathers, out pushing newspapers through doors, then off to school after a hurried breakfast. At the newsagents I worked from we had to pass by the darkened, but unlocked, main shop floor to get upstairs to where the papers were set out for us to sort for the rounds. The shop itself was very large and sold everything from papers to model kits and do-it-yourself items including paint.

I was really into making Air fix model kits of tanks and fighter planes and as I passed through the shop each morning, with the treasure trove of models inside beckoning me in, I was soon scheming how I could steal some of the model kits. I soon came up with a plan. It didn't take long as I had a very active and creative mind when it came to things like this.

On entering the shop through the back door, which was open for us paper boys to enter the shop, I simply ducked into the main sales room, to the right of the stairs. Once inside, in the dark, I carefully crept round to where the models were kept and I just picked up the one that I had pre-selected during the previous day's reconnaissance visit to see what I wanted to steal. I put the model box into a plastic shopping bag which I set down just outside of the doorway in the dark, then coolly went upstairs and calmly sorted my papers. I had told no one about my plan.

As I left, timing it to make sure I came down alone, I simply grabbed the bag with the goodies in, tucked it inside my paper delivery bag, and went on my way. As simple and easy as that. After that first time it became a regular event and I even stole to order for others. Easy money. My model collection grew rapidly and so I progressed onto taking the paint and brushes that I needed to make a really good job of the finished kits that I had made. The whole scam was simple and foolproof. Or so I thought.

Once I was very nearly caught red handed and it scared the life out of me, albeit briefly.

I had just gone inside the shop, intending to steal a model of a second world war battleship, the Bismarck, when I heard someone coming down the stairs, a pause, then the strip lights in the shop's ceiling flickering on above my head. My heart flickered as much as the lights, I'm telling you. I hid low behind some shelves of tinned house paints, holding my breath. I heard a low humming and I recognized the tune. It was the manager of the shop. He then began to whistle as he walked about. This was it. I was going to be caught out for certain. My mind raced to come up with an excuse for being in here. Luckily I hadn't taken the model yet, so I could possibly get away with it if caught. As quick as a flash I had an idea. I'd say that I saw a cat come in and I was just trying to find it and chase it out. It sounded a good idea at the time.

Then just as suddenly he had come in, he simply left turning the lights off as he went back out. I listened as he walked back up the stairs, keeping very still for several long minutes in case this was a trap. After a while I let out a long breath of relief. I promised myself there and then never to do this again.

Three days later, I had others in there with me, showing them the ropes, quite the big man now that I had survived the near miss of discovery. I now needed something bigger and grander to do to get more respect from the other lads.

Then came the idea for the sports shop job.

The inspiration came to me in a flash. Each morning my gang had to pass by the sports shop on Bridge Street, near the church, as we cycled out to our various paper rounds. At 5.30am it was always, without exception, deserted. It was very quiet and therefore very tempting. An ideal target for a smash and grab job.

There was always a good selection of sporting gear on view in the large glass windows of the shop. Golf clubs, football tops and balls. Everything you could imagine or want was there, ripe for the picking; including shot gun cartridges and that was what I really wanted. I had just discovered the joy of blowing things up, using a variety of homemade devices, mainly by means of fireworks. I had already got plans for a bomb with petrol and sand and elastic bands. Shotgun ammunition would be ideal addition, as would plenty of marbles or steel ball bearings from the shop.

So I came up with a plan. And a very good one at that, even if I say so myself! I put the idea to a few of the lads and I soon had a team ready for villainy.

We decided to all meet up by the church after getting our papers sorted out in the morning. This was to be our alibi if questioned as to where we were at the time. I would smash the window, and then all of us would hide in the church grounds to see if any alarms went off or if anyone came to see what the noise was. If no one came after a few minutes then we would run into the shop, grab what we wanted, then cycle away and carry on with the paper rounds, each of us disposing of the loot in some devious way. Simple and as sweet as a nut.

For a few days before the job we all went in the sports shop, one by one and at various times to see just what we wanted, a reconnaissance of sorts. We all felt professional, especially me. There was power in knowing that you were going to rob someone and they didn't know it. It felt very good. I was even pleasant to the owner of the shop, knowing exactly what I was going to do to him and his property.

The big day came and all of us were anxious and scared, though not one of us would dream of letting on to the others how we felt. It was more than obvious to me that the rest of the gang were worried. I just hoped that I didn't look like they did! That would never do.

By the time the four of us met at the church I was sweating, very excited and very much on edge. It was still pitch dark and a slight rain was falling. It was extremely quiet. I knew that we had to go through with this caper or else I would be made out to be a right fool. As much as I was scared I was more frightened of looking stupid if we didn't go through with this. Bad news travelled fast and I had a reputation to look after.

And there was no way that I was going to lose face in this.

I had placed a large chunk of concrete in the church grounds the night before. I knew that I had to be the one to throw it at the window. It was my plan and it was up to me to lead. The others were looking terrified and kept glancing up and down the street to see if anyone was about. I hoped, once again, that I didn't look like them. I tried my hardest to look cool and in control of things. To set a good example for the lads to follow!

Taking a deep breath I grabbed the concrete. "Here we go." I said and ran out from behind the wall and across the road, lobbed the concrete at the window as hard as I could, turned and literally dived over the churchyard wall even before the concrete hit the glass. The sound that followed me over the wall was the loudest thing I had ever heard in all my life. Like the crack of doom itself!

We all clung to the flint wall like soldiers under enemy fire, keeping as low as we could. I peered over the top. No alarms were ringing. A good sign.

No curtains were being pulled back from the flats up the road or any lights coming on. No one had been woken up by the sound of the crashing glass window. Good.

"Let's go!"

We raced across the road, jumped in through the gaping hole in the window and began to take the goods. It was a wild, wild three or four minutes, yet it seemed like hours when we were inside. We were all laughing like mad, the tension cracking through as we grabbed anything and everything, the carefully prepared plans for what we wanted to steal gone to pieces and just taking whatever came to hand.

Then we were gone, cycling away from the scene of the crime, perhaps on the strangest getaway vehicles in the history of crime; newspaper delivery bicycles!

I had got my shotgun cartridges, several boxes of them stashed in my bag. I also had a full set of golf clubs, complete with balls, in a proper golf bag slung round my neck as I wobbled away. I even had a tennis racquet sticking out of my jacket, a game that I had never played or thought about!

As per the plan, we all went to school, keeping as normal as possible, but all of us were on a wonderful high after what we had done. It was a great day for us. It was our secret.

But not for long!

CHAPTER FOUR.

The axe dropped on my neck as soon as I walked indoors that same day from school. I should've known something was up and felt the tremor in the force.

Mum stood in the kitchen with that look on her face I knew only too well. The one that said she was ready and primed for a confrontation. I immediately began to wonder what I had done and been caught out at.

"Can you explain what these are, Gary?" she pointed over to the dining room table. Stacked on the white tablecloth was a mountain of shotgun cartridge boxes! I suddenly went very cold. I didn't know what to say. I was caught by surprise. My expression must have been a picture. A dead giveaway to my guilt. I struggled for something to say.

"I found them." The lie sounded weak even to me but it was all that I could think of at the time. "I thought they would be safe with me." I shrugged my shoulders in an act of silky reasonableness, trying to inject a tone of indignation into my voice.

"You can tell that to the Police." Mum said. "They are on the way here."

The enormity of what was happening was horrendous. I considered running for it. I was in deep trouble and no mistake. I wondered how the others were doing, if any of them had been caught red handed like me. I suddenly felt like the Christmas turkey with a very exposed neck held down by a very firm hand.

The end result of it all was a police investigation that saw the four of us were taken to court and fined the huge sum of £40 each. That was a great deal of cash for us at the time. The other lads were suitably frightened by the events but I just found the whole thing a learning experience. I vowed next time to work alone as that way no one could drop you in it. Plus I would get to keep all the loot! You had to learn from your mistakes or there was no point in making them, was there? In my opinion anyways.

We were taken before the local Justice of the Peace, who just happened to be our headmaster from school, a certain Mr. Briggs. He was, I remember, an ex-Army officer. A good man, as I look back, but I didn't think so at the time.

"Have you learned your lesson, young man?" his voice was always loud and firm. Typical officer. He gave me a very hard look from his seat high in the courtroom.

"Yes sir." I thought I would play the game here for a change, pretending to be penitent. It wouldn't do any harm I decided, as I didn't mean it anyway.

"I don't want to see you before me ever again in this court. Is that clear?" I nodded, my eyes suitably lowered to the floor. He motioned to the courtroom door. "Then get out of here!" I left at great speed, a big grin all over my face but not until I was outside the building!

As well as the fine I was placed on probation for a period of time, under the watchful eye of a Mr. Boyles. He was a good sort and even got me on an outward-bound course, canoeing right across Scotland, from Fort William to Inverness, paddling all the way down the Caledonian Canal, taking in Loch Ness along the route. It was quite a time and did me the world of good. It fuelled my taste for adventure.

Various other misdemeanors took place over the years, but I was never caught again. I found that it was better, on the whole, to work alone. That way there was no one else to grass you up or to share any of the proceeds with.

The one time I made an exception to my rule very nearly ended in tragedy and death.

Not long after I had been taken back in at home I started staying out later and later, sometimes I would go to bed, saying my "Goodnights" to Mum, then sneak out to prowl around the St Martins Way estate, or even cross the River Thet and go to the notorious Abbey Farm estate.

When I was out at night I would move around the alleyways between the houses like a ghost, checking doors and trying car door handles to see if they were open. Stealing money left out for the milkman was also a favourite of mine, especially around the bungalows where the old folks lived. They were so trusting and had yet to catch up with modern times, simply leaving the milk money in the bottles with a little note. Easy money.

There was a certain addiction at being a predator out in the darkness of the night and I looked forward to the coming of the welcome cloak of shadows. On the odd occasion I would meet up with a few others and get up to all sorts as we roamed about, out of control. But I mostly went alone. Alone was better.

The culmination of this period of rebellion was when we broke into a house, not far from the town center. We didn't know who was there or even if there was anyone in the house. We just wanted cash or valuables. And to a practiced eye, the house looked very easy to enter.

After forcing a small side window, myself and another lad whom I shall call Colin, clambered inside the house, as silent as wraiths. We then opened the back door; easing back the bolts quietly and opening the door slightly, ready to make a quick getaway if needed. We sneaked around downstairs at first, straining in the dark to see what was there. We had forgotten to bring a torch with us such was the spontaneity of the whole event that night. There wasn't a great deal worth nicking downstairs, so we decided after a whispered conversation to go upstairs and see what was there. There had to be something of value somewhere in the house!

I went first, Colin followed. We both had knives in our hands, ready for use. Mine was a Bowie knife, with serrated edges on one side several inches long. It was a vicious looking thing. I honestly don't know for sure if I would have ever used it on someone in cold blood, but at the time I thought I would. The knife gave me a confidence to tackle anything or anyone.

As silent as shadows we checked each room, listening outside the bedroom doors for any sign of life inside, sounds like snoring, deep breathing or simply someone turning over in bed. When I was satisfied a room was empty I would go inside and check about. Colin kept guard outside on the landing.

After a few minutes of scrutiny all that was left to look into was one last bedroom. I could hear slight noises coming out of there, like labored breathing but not quite snoring. Someone was in there. I just knew that we had to go in there and check. It had to be done because that was where any cash or valuables were going to be. And I wanted them.

I was bricking it but there was no way that I was going to dry up in front of Colin, who was older and, so he thought, nastier than me. I wanted to be the top dog. I also had an inkling of how I was going to achieve that as well. And it would mean Collins downfall. Big time and possibly painfully as well.

I slowly opened the door and peered inside. There was better light in there as the curtains were slightly parted, allowing the glow from the streetlight outside in the precinct to come into the room.

There was an old lady asleep in a single bed and as I gently, cautiously, stepped into the room, a thought exploded into my head with an almost concussive force, "This is just like your Gran's room."

I hesitated in that second, not wanting to go any further into the room suddenly scared that she would wake up and see us there in the room. The thought about my Grans room had robbed me of the will to go ahead. But Colin was pressing up against me from behind, nudging me further inside. "Go on!" he hissed, right in my ear.

I went in.

The room was full of old stuff and I saw straightaway in the dim light that her purse was on the bedside cabinet only inches from her face. I reached for it, quickly opening it up and looking inside. It was stuffed with cash, all in notes. She must have of collected her pension the previous day. We'd hit the jackpot!

The old lady murmured something in her sleep- then suddenly woke up. I can still see, even now after all these years, the look of instant and absolute terror on her poor face, fear filling her features as she stared up at me as I stood over her in the bed.

"Don't do anything and you'll be alright." I spoke as softly as my tension filled voice would allow me. Both Colin and I wore masks over our faces with just slits in the fabric for our eyes to peer through. A sinister sight in daylight, let alone at 3am. "We're going now. Don't scream." I tried to inject a note of reasonableness into my voice, trying to calm her down.

Then Colin waved his knife at her as if to make the point that she would be hurt if she did scream, and in that second I felt as though I could've killed him for what he did. It was one thing to rob the old lady, but quite another to intentionally frighten her out of her wits as Colin did. It needed sorting and I decided there and then how I was going to do it. He was out of order and big time!

Within seconds we were gone from the house, through the un-bolted back door, running like crazy. To this day, in all honesty, I cannot remember exactly where it was.

We retreated to the top of Castle Hill, near to Nuns Bridges, which was an ancient earthen mound that was grandly called a castle. It was a good safe place to hide out. No one could come near us without being seen or heard, and was covered with bushes and small trees, masking us from sight even if anyone had been around at that time of day. Once there we broke into fits of laughter as the tension of the robbery was released. We had a smoke and talked about it as though it had been the Great Train Robbery.

The lads who had waited outside, acting as lookouts, hung onto our every word as Colin and I described in great detail the events, second by second, of what we had done and seen in the house.

"How much have we got?" Colin asked, nodding to the purse in my hands. To be honest I had never liked Colin in the time I had known him. Perhaps under different circumstances we could've been good friends. But not now. After the way he used his knife to scare the old lady on purpose I didn't want to give him anything. Except a good beating up.

"Not too much." I said. I had already taken out the majority of the notes from the purse as we had run from the house to Castle Hill and stuffed them deep in my pockets. I opened the purse to let the others see what was in there.

Colin grabbed the purse off me and poked inside." There was more than that inside." He gave me a hard stare. Tension crackled in the air like an approaching severe thunderstorm as Colin and I faced each other, knives in hand. "Where's it all gone, Gary?"

"That's all there was, mate." My voice was quiet and he had to lean forward to hear what I said. He was way too close to me now and in more danger than he realized.

"I saw much more than this." He waved the purse at me.

"Check me if you want." As I spoke I moved slightly to one side, coiled and ready to spring. As Colin opened his mouth to speak again, I attacked. Swiftly, decisively and so fast that I had my knife to his neck, my right foot behind his leg tripping him backwards, then down on his face onto the muddy ground, the razor sharp knife tip right against his skin before he knew what had hit him. I grabbed his hair, pulling back his head, exposing his neck for the knife. All the anger and hate in me welled up in me and yet, strange as it may sound, I was as cold and controlled as could be. It scared even me in that moment. If he had of fought back I would have cut his throat. No hesitation.

And he knew it!

The other lads just watched in terror at the scene before them, eyes wide in fear, keeping well clear.

It was a hinge point in my life, where events could've gone either way. For good or for bad. There have been many of these times in my life, a tipping point of sorts.

As Colin literally cried in fear, begging me not to hurt him, sobbing like a little girl, I cut him slightly just enough to draw blood, and then I let him go. I also handed him the purse as he stood up. "Keep the lot!" with that I walked off, away from the gang. I had proved my point and was top dog. No one was going to mess with me when word got out of what had just happened. And get out it would. I was shaking from head to foot at what had so nearly happened, how I could've killed Colin. The adrenaline rush was great!

Life or death had been a heartbeat away. And boy, did it feel good!!

Knives were to feature largely in my life in later years, getting me into trouble, quite seriously on one occasion.

Looking back now I can see how God had had His hand on my life, even when I had no idea that He even existed, steering my life towards a point in time when I could have the chance to hear of who He was. And that He wanted to meet with me as well. My life was spared on more than one occasion.

The one immediate incident that comes to mind was when I was about ten. We were living in Norwich and were about to go away for a few days holiday. A friend was coming to pick us up in a car. I was excited as could possibly be about the trip and had been waiting around the front of the house for the first sight of the car. As I waited I got bored and so ran quickly round the side of the house, heading for the back door, when I tripped and fell headlong right onto an old pram wheel that I had been intending to use as part of a go-cart. The metal spokes from the wheel were broken and pointing straight up into the air, and I fell onto one of them, and the thin metal spoke went right through my neck, missing the windpipe and spinal cord by millimeters. I had somehow supported my whole weight as I fell on my hands. Looking back it was an impossible moment. It was as though I had just stopped dead, and lay there, impaled on the spokes. The angels had been working overtime that day!

Mum found me, alerted by the terrified screams of my sister, and since we couldn't afford a telephone and the nearest call box was some distance away from us, Mum simply carried me to the nearest bus stop, figuring it would be quicker to go by bus than waiting for an ambulance to come.

The big red bus came and the conductor took one look at me, yelled to the driver to head for the Accident and Emergency, and so I was rushed to hospital on a big red double decker bus! This has to be a first in arriving at hospital in an emergency. I was nearly unconscious by the time we arrived and the sight of the white-jacketed hospital porter coming for me was frightening. I thought maybe it was an angel and that I was dying. The whole episode even made the local papers complete with photographs!

There was one other time that springs to mind when I was very nearly killed, and this again involved a knife. Surprise, surprise!

I was down on my knees when a knife was thrown at me. As it tumbled through the air, coming straight at my head, I knew without a doubt that it was going to hit me right in the face. It was a perfect throw and, being on one knee, there was no way that I could avoid it. I was off balance, big time!

I can remember thinking how good a throw it was, when I was suddenly and violently pushed sideways to the left, the knife grazing past my face, so close I could feel the rush of moving air, landing somewhere behind me. I was amazed at the time at what had happened and I couldn't understand how it had missed, just that it had.

The Angels were once again working overtime that day on my behalf!

The sad thing about the incident was that it had been my girlfriend who had thrown the knife at me!

I certainly knew how to pick them!

CHAPTER FIVE.

It seemed as though my entire life was full of opposites.

On the one hand I was getting uncontrollable, doing exactly as I pleased, when I pleased, getting up and into all kinds of scrapes and situations without any concern for those I affected or hurt in the process

Yet there was another side to me; a calmer more normal and youthful character that competed with the darker side for dominance all the time. I knew the good that I should be doing and was capable of, but the dark side of the force seemed stronger, vying for supremacy, all very Star Wars. I was constantly aware of this tension within me all the time, pulling and tearing at me, like some invisible gravitational force clutching me in its giants hand intent on ripping me apart from within.

I had joined the local Air Training Corps, an organization for both girls and boys that teach the basic of life in the Royal Air Force. Disciplines like marching and wearing a uniform and doing as told were part and parcel of ATC life. The Army has the Army Cadet Force and the Royal Navy has the Sea Cadets and is a training organization that do the same job.

I enjoyed being a part of the ATC. I learned to wear the uniform with pride and enjoyed the time and effort it took to look good. I also took great pleasure at marching and seemed to excel. It appeared for a while as though the good side of me was winning through and I was actually enjoying my life.

Very soon I was taking and passing exams on the theory of flight and various other new things I was learning in the teaching lessons on parade nights. I actually took to it all better than my schoolwork and was soon gaining very good grades. I soon I came to the notice of Warrant Officer Alerton, who was responsible for 1109 squadrons drum and bugle marching band that was just being formed. It was fun learning to play a bugle, and then I took on the snare drums. I even had a go at the bass drum, reminding me so much of the Salvation Army band that I had loved so much as a little boy. I gave that big bass drum some hard use gaining some top class blisters in the process! Boy, did they hurt but the fun I had way outweighed the hurt!

Very quickly it was decided by Mr. Alerton that I should be the Drum Major of the band, a very important and responsible role in any marching band. The Drum Major keeps the band heading in the right direction and marches at the head swinging the mace as he leads the way. I remember not long after I was asked to do this I saw the Queen's birthday parade on the television and was extremely impressed when I saw the band of the Brigade of Guards. I studied the drum major as if my life depended upon it. I decided that I was going to be as good as they were! For once I had a purpose in my life and I jumped in with both feet, determined to be the very best that I could be no matter what it took for me to do it. I was single minded and focused.

I was nearly always the first to be at the training hut on the small RAF Barn ham camp just outside of Thetford. Sometimes I would even walk there across the common if the coach were late, as I would worry that it wouldn't turn up. It was great to have a purpose in life. And even better in many ways was that I was mixing with reasonably normal boys of my own age, who would never dream of getting involved with many of the things that I was. Being normal was as foreign as possible to be but somehow I fitted right in.

Mr. Alerton gave me great encouragement and I blossomed under the role I had. I was determined to be the best I could and it showed in the way that I dealt with the other lads. Promotion soon followed as I sat and passed basic exams in every subject placed before me. As the band improved we were entered into marching band competitions and even won a few minor events. We even travelled once to London to take part in the huge Lord Mayors procession. It took three hours to complete the route in the sweltering heat of that summer's day but we were all so proud to be taking part. I vividly remember being so tired at the end of the day that I could hardly speak but was bulging with pride at having been a part of the day.

But the crowning glory, however, was when we were invited to take part in an episode of Dad's Army, a comedy program that was the nation's favorite for many, many years in this country.

The filming location was near to Thetford in Norfolk and it was a glorious sunny day as we drove out to the film site on a coach. All of us were excited and really looking forward to meeting the stars of the show and as the days went on we met them all, getting autographs from them and having a real good laugh.

People like Arthur Low who played the loveable Captain Mainwaring. John Mesurier as Sgt Wilson. Ian Lavender as the foolish Private Pike. Edward Sinclair as the Verger. And so on and all were household names.

They were happy, for the most past, to chat to us in between filming and we were thrilled and a little awed that these men would take them time to simply chat with us boys.

Our role for the show was to dress up as the Sea Scouts band that was taking part in the fictional town of Warming-ton-on-Sea's annual St Georges day fete. We were given Sea Scout uniforms from the Second World War period to look the part and were even given haircuts to match as well! All very smart indeed.

We had to march about with the Verger leading us around the large town green, playing the drums and bugles, then to March by the podium where the town mayor was to take the salute. In the script the Verger was to trip and nearly fall over as we passed by the saluting podium and there was much laughter as we filmed the shot several times to get it just right. It was a really happy time with a huge amount of laughter. There I was, fifteen years old and having the time of my life. Life was suddenly and gloriously good as if nothing bad had ever happened to me in my entire life.

Later on we also had to be the legs in the dragon as battle commenced between Captain Mainwaring, who was dressed as St George, and the dragon. At one stage we had to stop filming as the smoke machine inside the dragon's head went haywire and filled the inside of the costume with smoke! We had to abandon ship, coughing and spluttering, hugely amused by it all.

Many years later I used to tell my friends and especially my two sons, Barney and Jacob, what I had done that day. But it was obvious that no one really believed me and it wasn't until there was a re-run of all the old episodes that my program was shown. And there I was, fifteen years old and quite skinny and with exceptionally white legs! What a star! My two sons roared with laughter at seeing their Dad on the TV.

For some months my life was going well. I hadn't been in any major trouble and my schoolwork was as good as it was ever going to get, and to cap it all I was getting on well in the ATC. I was even nice, on occasion, to Mum and Bob.

Then one night as I came home for some tea I heard Mum crying. I went into the kitchen to see what the matter was. I'd never heard her crying much in all of my life. It took a great deal to scare me, but I was very alarmed at the sound. I knew there had to be something really bad for mum to be like this.

I stood in the doorway. "What's wrong, Mum?" and as I asked there was a terrible sinking feeling in my stomach, like a sudden drop in an elevator.

"Granddad died today." Was all she could say. She burst back into floods of tears, her back to me as she stood at the sink, shoulders heaving with emotion at the death of her Dad.

My whole world fell apart in that moment. Nothing could have prepared me for this. My Granddad was one of the most vital people in my life. Now he was gone, snatched away.

I didn't know what to do so I just ran and ran, weeping and crying as I did, not caring who saw me. I headed into the forest to howl at the moon.

Pictures and memories of all the years of playing together came flooding back, washing over me like a dam bursting, unstoppable and intent on causing damage.

Of all the times we had played darts together for long hours at a time in the back garden. Of playing snap in the front room. Of me helping out in the garden digging and carrying in vegetables for him. Of the bonfires late at night, laughing and just glad to be in each other's company. Of just sitting together, comfortable at being close on the sofa and watching the television. Of rummaging through the big shed in the garden, curious as to what I would find in there. Of that peculiar smell of his tobacco as he rolled his cigarettes. Of his big rough hands and kind words for me.

Gone forever.

No goodbyes and not even the chance to tell Granddad one last time how much I loved him.

The news of my granddads death had hit me so very badly it was hard to explain how I felt, even now, these long years after. Not only was he my beloved granddad but he was, in many ways, as close to a Dad as I was ever going to have in this life and I doted on him.

All I have of my granddad Ernie was good memories when he took the trouble to spend enormous amounts of time with this little bastard boy, who no one else really wanted to know. I knew that he loved me by the way he acted.

We had great times spent together in that long garden in common lane tending the food grown there, often working side by side, and the gardening spade he used taller than me. I remember being so proud the day I was taller than the wooden handle.

Then there was the fun of eating the raw tomatoes stolen from his big glass greenhouse and later on, when slightly older, sneaking out his bottles of homemade beer and wine! I was getting tipsy aged 11 years and up.

Granddad also took the time to help me with my model making efforts using Air-fix kits bought locally. I made world war two planes, tanks, and ships and then spent endless hours embarking on dangerous adventures to win battles against insurmountable odds, somehow always pulling through! Looking back it was a kind of training for how most of my life has been; taking on big tasks and somehow coming through.

Although it was my grandmother I loved with all of my heart, granddad was right up there but in a different kind of way.

I respected him and lived in a kind of awe of him and the way the he answered the endless line of questions I always seemed to have on just about every subject under the sun.

Sunday afternoons was my favorite times when there was nearly always a cowboy film on, often of John Wayne, and I would sit with granddad and thoroughly enjoy the film, adding to the films soundtrack with my own brand of special effects as I backed up the hero with my little plastic toy six guns !

So when the news of his death arrived it really seemed as if my entire life came to a crashing halt.

For some time before his death I had been very low moods, depressed possibly, as it seemed that the very things I didn't want to do I actually ended up doing. It was if my entire life was in a downward spiral and that unseen hands controlled my every move like some puppet on a string.

Unknown to anyone I actually hated myself, blaming the fact that I didn't have a dad on myself as if, somehow, it was my entire fault. It was a stupid, unreasonable way to think but that was how I felt. Useless and unwanted and one of life's rejects.

For long, long months my mind seemed to be filled with nasty, black thoughts of ending my life. I was 15 and already fed up with life and was looking for a way out.

Although I had a girlfriend of sorts at the time, it was never a chatty sort of relationship and I would have never dreamed of talking to granny about what was going on in my head. That would've worried her so I kept all of it bottled up, fermenting away as the anger and hurt built up ready to explode. Trouble wasn't far away.

For long days I would dream up ways of ending my life, even making detailed notes of the time, place and how I would do it. I had several goodbye letters penned away and ready to be posted or left behind. To be honest there was a kind of calmness about it all as if I at least had this little bit of control over what happened to me.

In the end my best, most reliable way of killing myself was perhaps the most simple as well.

So just after lunch one Saturday afternoon, I had a shower, changed my clothes, wrote a brief farewell note to mum and granny and left them on my pillow, and headed off, alone as usual, deep into Thetford forest; my death planned and looked forwards too.

The forest had always been my favorite place to be, night or day, no matter the season or weather. There was something natural about the solitude and grandness of the trees that had captured my heart.

Cutting through the forest was the main train track leading east towards Norwich and west towards Kings Lynn and it was a mainly regional train service
And one I had been on so many times before. I loved train journeys.

Very often I had sat at the edge of the trees watching the trains speed past and on two separate occasions I had even tried to derail the locomotives by dragging into the forest heavy concrete posts and laying them on the railway tracks. I was thoroughly thrilled when one train driver spotted the posts and slammed on the brakes. No one knew I was just yards away camouflaged in the woods and I enjoyed watching the mayhem that I caused by my mad actions.

I had selected several days before a particular spot and decided that I would simply wait in the woods until the trains was at its fastest; then simply walk out and step in front of the train, giving the driver no time to stop. I figured it would be a quick way to die and I could stand there, eyes closed, and wait the few seconds for oblivion to greet me.

As simple as that. My useless life snuffed out. Easy.

It was a very cold afternoon as I sat there on the edge of the tree-line but it didn't bother me as I was a cold weather person anyway. I had no idea when the next train was due so I just listened to the familiar sounds of the wildlife moving about around me. A deer sauntered past me, totally unaware of my presence, within touching distance and for some strange reason I felt envious of that creature.

No problems, no worries. Just living, eating, and dying in the forests. A simple life.

A light rain began to fall, almost like a fine mist, and it brought with it that beautiful freshness that feels as if the very oxygen had been cleansed by the rain. The freshness of the pine trees was incredible and I knew that I would miss all this when I died.

Tears stung my eyes, hot and salty, as I sensed the enormity of what I was there to do. An awful chest ripping sadness gripped me like a giant's fist. I knew that my granny would be upset by news of my death and I began to sob even more at the thought of never seeing her again until I thought that my heart was going to burst and cause serious internal damage. A one point I even doubled up on the ground, such was the pain of it all.

There was one word that kept coming to my lips all the time this was happening and was one I had no answer to; perhaps no one did.

It was the word WHY?

I awoke with a start, cold, stiff and very wet, surprised that I had drifted off to sleep in the undergrowth. The rain had picked up and was falling in solid sheets of cold water. I was soaked right to the bone and was shivering with the cold; yet my resolve to go through with it all hadn't dampened. My mind was set.

I felt, rather than heard, the sound of a train approaching, so I stood up shaking now with both cold and a sudden hot flush of fear, and stumbled forwards towards the train tracks, twin dark lines in the gathering gloom. I felt strangely detached from it all as if I was watching someone else walking to their death; a spectator to the obscene.

I lay down next to the metal tracks, letting my fingers rest on the cold wet metal, feeling the vibrations tingle my fingertips; then I simply placed my left ear down on the track, hearing and feeling my death approaching. I wondered if I should just lie here, keeping still and just let the train wheels take my head off. It wouldn't take any effort to do, just close my eyes and die.

There was a lovely calmness washing over me that I hadn't felt for so very long and maybe it was because I was now in control of things and this was my final act, my last defined decision.

I suddenly felt scared and more afraid in that moment than at any other time in my entire life; and wondered yet again why life had been so unfair to me. I began to cry.

The train was very loud now and I lifted my head and watched as the big locomotive came round the long curve about half kilometer away, edging round like some huge metal reptilian executioner.

Absently I thought it would only take a few more seconds for the train to hit me, again that awful feeling of total detachment from everything around me, like looking in from the outside on events. All my life I had felt on the outside of things, as if I couldn't touch a single living person; as if I was immune to emotion.

I closed my eyes, took a quick deep breath and decided that I would rather face the monster head on, my last act of courage as I died; I jumped up and stepped into the middle of the twin tracks, gravel crunching underfoot.

The driver caught sight of me, just seconds away and I could see the wide O shape of his shocked open mouth, the burst of terror and stunned look to his eyes as I stood there , knowing he couldn't stop in time.

I looked up into his face - and calmly side stepped off the rails feeling the whip-like percussion as the train zipped past behind me, that terrible screeching of iron wheels as the driver slammed the brakes on, the driver unaware that he hadn't hit me.

Without as much as a backwards glance I walked back into the forest, merging with the familiar and headed home.

I can't explain, even to this day as I sit here writing this story, just what made me step aside in those last appalling seconds before the train hit. Certainly it wasn't any conscious decision to live.

All I know for sure was that the day was a nasty one and just a bit too much to bear.

I just wish that there had of been someone to talk to. A Christian perhaps?

✕⟩

Some weeks after Granddad's death and the train incident I was still thoroughly depressed, crying constantly and just didn't know what to do with myself. However, I woke up one morning and decided, there and then, that I would go to Rome, Italy. I don't know why I thought this, but I did. It just seemed like a good idea at the time.

So I packed my rucksack, filled it with goodies from the kitchen and off I went. All I had was about £10 with me and that was it. I hitchhiked down to Dover, bought a temporary British passport from a post office and went across to France. From there I thumbed it all the way to Rome, using just my school atlas as a map, in just three days. I walked the last few miles into the city, remembering history lessons about the famous Roman Legions as they victoriously entered Rome after some far off conquest. It felt as though I was walking, quite literally, in their footsteps.

I went to see the Vatican and St Peters Square. I had no religious reasons for going there, just simple curiosity as I had seen it on the TV. I was fascinated by the whole place especially the massive water fountains in the middle of the huge square, from which I drank. I remember that the water was very cool and tasty. Thousands and thousands of people were in the square that day, wandering around and taking pictures, the place buzzing with sound. But I was all alone in the crowds as I strolled about. Like standing inside a goldfish bowl, staring out.

As night came I wondered where I could sleep rough, and I decided that one of the large stone benches in the Vatican City would do. As I unrolled my sleeping bag a priest stopped and asked if I was all right. He spoke English and told me that I would be safe enough to sleep on the bench. He gave me his word to this effect and then he handed me a small card with his name on it if I should have any trouble. I thanked him, took off my walking boots and lay down under a clear Roman sky.

I slept well that night.

✕⟩

The day I left school was the day that I officially moved out from home. Bob had found me some lodgings in a private home for £15 a week. It was a bit of a dump but seemed good to me at the time. I had a single room to myself and all my meals included. Best of all, I was left alone to come and go as I pleased.

Bob helped me to move there and he even paid for the first weeks rent for me. He was a good guy.

Looking back I often feel ashamed of the way that I treated Bob. He loved my mum and was willing to take on 3 children that were not his own, something that I admire in any man whose done that. He was a good man once I got to know him.

Soon I had another sister, Rachel, the product of his marriage to my Mum.

My first job on leaving school was at a factory called Danepak, the bacon people. I worked in the print room, where they printed the boxes that the bacon was packed in. I nearly jacked the job in after just a few hours. I was still upset by Granddads death and he was all I could think about. People don't realize that young people can be depressed, upset and confused by life.

After four weeks I jacked it in and took a job at another factory, packing frozen chickens into boxes. Factory work is deadly boring, repetitious and noisy. I decided this was not the life for me. I had friends who loved factory work and God bless them all, but it was not for me.

However, I kept working since it was good to have a steady flow of cash coming in, honestly gained. I was keeping out of trouble for the most part. Well, I wasn't getting caught anyway!

I began to wonder if there was any more to life than just all of this. I was 16 years old and already seriously fed up with life and what it had to offer me. Deep dark feelings of gloom threatened to drown me and it was hard to keep my spirits up most of the time. It was a real battle against the darkness.

My then girlfriend and her mother had recently become Catholics and so one Sunday I decided to attend with them and to see what was what. Church had never, ever, featured in my life, apart from the odd wedding and funeral.

So I went along. The service could've been in ancient Greek for all I could understand of it. But I saw that all of those who attended the service were very sincere in their beliefs. I saw the change in my girlfriend straight away. But religion wasn't for me. It was for old ladies and the weak. Besides, being in the church made me feel very guilty for some reason that day, as if I was missing out on something good.

The only time before that I had had any contact with the church was when my sister, Debbie and I, were invited on a trip for underprivileged children to the beach at Lowestoft. I was about ten years old. It was a very hot day and it was nice for the two of us to be there. At lunchtime, as everyone settled down on the sand to eat his or her pack lunches, disaster struck us both!

The top of the lemonade bottle had come undone unbeknown to us and had poured out over all of our sandwiches, soaking them. We now had nothing to eat. I wouldn't ask anyone for something to eat and I remember being utterly crushed by the fact that Debbie was going hungry. No one seemed to notice us, even though we had been invited along with many others. We both sat there on the beach, surrounded by others on the trip, as though we were invisible. What should've been a happy day quickly out turned nasty for us both.

So we just sat there while others ate their food and were filled. The one saving grace of the day was that later towards the end of the trip we all had a fish and chip dinner, before heading back to Norwich. We were both famished by that time.

What strikes me as I write this is that no one in my early life had shared the good news of Jesus with my family or me.

Where were all the Christians?

Why had no one ever told me about Jesus? All the churches around this land and not one person, ever, had taken the time or energy to tell us.

It makes you wonder doesn't it?

I just knew that there had to be more to life than just day-to-day existence. If not then what was the point to it all?

Surely there has to be some excitement in life, without having to resort to crime to get the buzz?

One Saturday afternoon I was downtown in Thetford, hanging around, considering going shoplifting. As I stood in the precinct I caught sight of a soldier walking down the slope towards me. I had seen thousands over the years since the big Army training grounds are not far from Thetford and they were often on maneuvers.

But there was something about this soldier that caught my attention. Tall, big built, he walked along as though he owned the place. There was an air of confidence about him that drew me to him. He was dressed in camouflage gear and looked like a man you wouldn't want to mess with. He had a big droopy moustache, which suited him perfectly. I could see others around me glancing at him as he passed by.

As he moved by me, he looked straight at me and nodded. I nodded back. "Alright, mate" he said.

"Yeah." I managed to say. And that was that.

I was going to be a soldier!

CHAPTER SIX

The train journey from Thetford's small and very cold British Rail (as it was then called) station was boring, yet full of tension and excitement at the same time.

Mum and Bob had come to the station to see me off. I had joked that they were only there to make sure that I actually left as promised. I was probably closer to the truth than I knew in all honesty. Truth hurts.

My final destination that day was to be Sutton Cold field, near Birmingham, and the Army base there where potential British Army recruits were tested both physically and mentally to see if they met the basic requirements. If they were successful then they would go onto the regiments they had enlisted in, where they would be trained to be professional soldiers in the British Army.

I had gone some weeks before to the Army careers information office in the small cathedral town of Bury St Edmunds and applied to join as a full time soldier. After some elementary tests a week later, followed by a basic medical checkup, I had been formally accepted as a potential soldier. I had taken the Queens shilling after swearing allegiance to Her Majesty Queen Elizabeth, and was to be trained, if accepted, in the art of modern infantry soldering with the Royal Engineers. I had thought about joining the Royal Anglian Regiment, which was the local Army Regiment. My great grandfather had served with the Royal Norfolk regiment in the Boer war, as had various other family members over the years. His uniform is still kept in the Beccles museum, along with some medals from his service fighting in the Sudan and South Africa.

A highlight of my joining up day had been having a pint of beer in a small pub next door to the Army office. I had just sworn allegiance to Her Majesty the Queen and felt as though I could take on the world and win. The pub was called the Walnut and was reputedly the smallest pub in England. It seemed big enough to me that day as the beer flowed down my neck!

The sergeant who had taken me there told me story after story of his exploits far and wide, serving as a British soldier in some difficult and dangerous places. Looking back now I wonder how much was just plain old big talk, but at the time it was so very real to me. I was being accepted into a man's world and it felt good. Really good.

I had been hooked on joining ever since seeing that soldier back in Thetford and was determined to get in no matter what the cost. And here I was, drinking beer, almost a soldier.

Mum and Bob had been more than pleased with me, surprised that I was doing something to better myself. I had seen Granny in Beccles the day before leaving and that was very hard for both of us. We had grown even closer since Granddad's death and I felt very responsible for her now. I had been in tears on the bus back to Thetford. A tough guy like me, crying. Unheard of.

So here I was, making the break from all that I was familiar with, heading into the unknown.

Birmingham train station was a shock to me. The sheer size of the place and the speed that people moved about. I eventually found the right platform for the smaller commuter train that went out to Sutton Cold field.

As I boarded the train I couldn't help but notice that there were other young men like myself, suitcases in hand, looking worried for the most part, but trying not to. A few lads knew each other and the banter was very loud. But for the most part it was an individual journey, each to his own thoughts and fears. Some of the lads honestly looked scared to death. A couple appeared on the point of tears, obviously the first time away from home for them. I decided to keep away from them. Fear can be almost like a nasty rash that can be caught.

On arrival at Sutton station a large number of uniformed soldiers met us, holding clipboards, and very smartly turned out. As we gathered on the platform in a large untidy group, names were called out and ticked off as we responded. Once done we were led out and into the car park where several buses waited for us to transport us to the main camp.

The next three days were a blur of tests, activities, and lectures, as we were checked out to see if we were up to serving in the world's most professional army. During meal times there was cacophony of accents from just about every corner of the British Isles. It was the first time in my life I had heard some of them. I once tried to have a conversation with a lad from Glasgow but had to give it up after only a few short minutes as I needed an interpreter to understand what he was saying. He ended up in the Black Watch regiment, one of the toughest of them all.

Although I had enlisted into the Royal Engineers, there was nothing firm about it. It was simply a case that you had to have something down on the forms before you go. As the tests progressed we were marked and scores were given. The higher the scores you made, the more technical a job you could apply for.

Lectures were given en bloc on the many and varied roles within the modern British Army. An extremely smart officer, wearing a red cap, approached me one afternoon after one of the lectures. I knew that he was a Military Policeman.

"What regiment are you going for, young man?" he asked.

"Royal Engineers, sir." I stood at attention as I spoke to him, my training in the Air Training Corps kicking in. I could see he was impressed with me.

"I'd say that you would be wasted there, son." He said. "The size of you and your obvious good attitude, I'd say that we need a big man like you in the Corps of Royal Military Police. What do you think about that?"

I was quite impressed that he had called me a man!

He went on to explain about the better pay, the instant promotion to Lance Corporal (one step above Private, the lowest of the low). There would also be better accommodation. Looking back now I can see that it was a first class sales pitch. The reason Military Policemen have better accommodation is that no one likes them, to put it bluntly.

He made it sound so good. He failed to mention, however, that the RMP's are actually the most hated unit in the entire army! The RMP's have to keep discipline and police the army, carrying out investigations and so on.

The thought of being a policeman didn't have a great deal of appeal to me. I have a brief chuckle at what my mates would say about me, Gary Moore, being a copper!

I was undecided and it must have shown.

"There's always plenty of scraping." He joked.

And that decided me!

I was in!

Snatched from the fire.

CHAPTER SEVEN

The Royal Military Police Training Centre (R.M.P.T.C.) was based at Roussillon barracks in the town of Chichester, East Sussex and it was exactly the way I had pictured it would be. I had seen a few military bases in my time and they were all built basically the same way, maybe even designed by the same anonymous architect with a serious lack of imagination.

There were large brick-built very uniform buildings intersected with pathways, spotless and litter free, with well-kept and low cut green grass areas filing in the spaces in between upon which a human foot never trod. No one ever dared to walk on military grass. Everything very ordered and in its place. All those out in the sunshine of the morning moved about with purpose and aim, marching alone or as a group. Nothing causal ever happened on a British Army camp. Everything was done by the numbers and very ordered.

On arrival at the train station at Chichester, just a stone's throw away from the infamous Globe Public House, we had been met, then been driven in four ton Lorries to the R.M.P.T.C. and deposited right beside the main lecture hall, suitcases dumped outside. The hall was full of new recruits and the staff that were going to train us. The noise level was muted, everyone there unsure of what was going to happen. Then a rather distinguished looking officer walked into the hall and the Regimental Sergeant Major (RSM) called us to attention in a booming voice that we would all get to know and hate over the coming months. This officer was the Commanding Officer (CO) of the RMP and he was to introduce us to life within the Corps. He gave us what is traditionally called 'The Talk'. Every new intake has a variation of his speech.

"By the end of this course, those of you who survive the rigors of the training will be members of an elite corps within the British Army." He explained at length exactly what the training was going to entail. It sounded somewhat harder than they told me back at Sutton Coldfield. I wasn't that worried but I did have a nagging sense of foreboding that trouble of sorts was looming just over the horizon, as yet unseen. Various other junior officers gave short talks about what was to happen to us as the months progressed. To me it sounded great and I couldn't wait to get started. As I glanced around at the other lads I felt the same sense of eagerness flowing like electricity in the room.

After 'The Talk' was over we were taken, almost like an all-male tourist group, over to our accommodation block that was to be our home for the next few months as we went through basic training, and were assigned rooms. My room held eleven other lads and the first thing we did was to pick a bed and dump our suitcases on top. Apart from the bed there was a wardrobe and small bedside locker, all very military and functional. This was my new home and it looked all right to me.

I knew none of the other lads and as we unpacked we began to chat, exchanging names and where we were from. Next to me was a young man from Jersey with a distinctive French accent. He was soon known simply as Frenchy, even to the training staff. To my other side, was a lad with a Liverpool accent so thick that you could spread it with a knife. He was, of course, called Scouse.

The next few hours were a blur of ordered activity as we were walked across to the quartermaster's stores and issued with all the kit that we would need for our basic training. From boots to mess tins and cutlery, camouflage jackets and trousers, PT shorts and trainers, tooth brushes and cleaning kit, right down to some rather awful green underpants! Everything you could think of was provided and had to be signed for. I don't think that I had ever seen so many forms needing my signature.

Following a trip back to the barracks to drop off our kit it was off to the medical Centre for a reasonably comprehensive examination by the camp doctor with the famous, "cough please". More questions and the inevitable forms to be signed.

The start of the course proper was still three days away, since we arrived on a Friday morning and so we had a breathing space to get settled in and to begin to find our way about the camp. We also went into Chichester town and sampled a few pints of beer at the Globe pub. Very nice indeed.

A small team of Non-commissioned officers (NCOs) were assigned to us as the training staff for our basic training course. For the first few days as we settled in they seemed like normal human beings as they introduced themselves to us and were very friendly and chatty, answering all of the many and varied questions we had about what was going to happen during the training. However, we soon learned to dread the sound of their voices once training was underway. They soon turned out to be less than human to us.

One man in particular stood out over all the others and that was a certain Staff Sergeant Lamont, a huge bear of a man. He looked nasty, especially when he smiled, and just by being in close proximity was more than enough to strike fear into the bravest of us. He was a good man for all that.

Monday and Day one of basic training arrived and I thought that the end of the world had come upon me, it was that bad!

0600hrs and the doors to the accommodation block were slung open and the training staff NCOs burst in, shouting and screaming at the top of their voices, sending us all, including me, into a blind panic. We'd had no idea this was going to happen. One lad even burst into tears, such was the shock of that first morning as the Army began to break us down, and ready to build we back up into the soldiers they needed. It was a tough brutal process but it was needed.

In minutes we were dressed in PT shorts and t-shirts and herded outside and off for a two mile run around the outside of the camp, along public roads, yelled at every meter of the run by the staff. It was a real shock to the system exercising at that unearthly hour, and once back, and showered, it was off to breakfast. Several lads couldn't face food after the run and were told, in no uncertain terms, that it was an offence under Army Regulations to miss breakfast. Big fry-ups were the usual.

That first week was one of shock and awe as we were bombarded with so much information that it was impossible to take it all in. First we learnt one of the very basics of soldering and that was cleanliness. Lessons on how to iron our clothes to army standards was a major obstacle to many of us. Hours were spent on bulling up our parade boots to a mirror like sheen until we could see our faces on the toecap. Some of the younger lads even had to be shown how to shave properly, others how to wash! All very basic but in fact essential to life in the armed forces.

One major session was spent on teaching us exactly how our uniform lockers were to be laid out. Everything had to be perfect with shirts and all items of clothing arranged in exact order, or else the sky would fall on us. Beds were made up to specific instructions and had to be followed as the staff used rulers to measure what we had done. It took ages to do and some lads even took to sleeping on the floor at night to save time making up the bed packs in the morning.

I had two major advantages over many of the others; one was that I already knew how to wear a uniform from my time with the Air Cadets and was comfortable with the fact. The other was that I knew all about marching and was competent on the parade ground having been thoroughly grounded by hours spent marching, again with the Air cadets. I breathed a silent prayer of thanks for this.

The first two weeks were spent, hour after hour, learning to march as an intake on the huge drill square under the ever-watchful eye of Staff Lamont and others. Many of the lads had great trouble and some seemed as though they had two left feet with a serious lack of coordination between brain and feet. They received some heavy-duty in the face shouting from the Drill Instructors. Since these men were used to training soldiers from the Brigade of Guards, they had almost insurmountable standards for us to achieve and let us know that we were useless in no uncertain terms and language.

As I had no such trouble I was able to pass on some advice in the evenings or at breaks in the program. I hadn't quite got the hang of ironing and so someone helped me. Slowly but very surely we began to mold together as a group, changing from individuals from varied and diverse backgrounds, to a single entity that began to rely on each other's help just to make it through the day.

Although the course was harsh, especially the physical training side of things, I soon found that I was in my element, almost as though I had been born to soldier, created for one purpose only, and was thoroughly enjoying myself.

Many others, however, soon found out that the opposite was true for them. Week by week familiar faces would suddenly disappear from the barrack rooms, sometimes with little or no notice that they were leaving. For some it was a blessed relief and they would openly admit that they had made a big mistake in ever joining in the first place. I couldn't understand this first group. Why anyone would want to leave of their own accord was beyond me. I had no time for quitters as I was resolved to stick it out no matter. There was a tenacity about my surviving the training.

However, others hung their heads in shame as they were kicked off the course for not being suitable, for a variety of reasons. For these ones it was a bitter pill and I genuinely felt sorry for them, but it only hardened my resolve that no way was I going to be 'binned', a term used for being kicked out. This was a constant threat hanging over each and every one of us that if we didn't do well and pass each section of the training course we would be history. For those who were trying hard, this was unthinkable, and as friendships were forged in those tough weeks, we turned from boys to men in the fire of affliction.

Soon the original 50 was down to 40, then to 30 of the original intake that had arrived just a few weeks previous.

My biggest personal challenge came when Staff Lamont took a serious dislike to me. Because of my size, as one of the largest in the intake, he would always seem to pick on me, no matter what I did, getting right in my face. His favorite action was to prod me in the chest, winding me up, trying to break me. Even to this day I don't like being prodded and won't take it from anyone.

Several times Lamont ripped up my bed pack, which had taken me a great deal of time and effort to get just right, and took immense delight in scattering my clothes and kit from the locker all over the floor. His favorite wind up, however, was to step right on the highly polished toecaps of my drill boots, ruining them. This would mean several hours that night to bring them back up to scratch once again, before the next morning inspection. It was a soul-destroying work, especially when tired and having so many other things to do as well.

It seemed as though he was constantly goading me to the point that the other lads were very aware of what was happening. Such was the hassle he gave me that a couple of the lads suggested we have a word with our training officer about it, as it was verging on the point of bullying. I said no to this, as I wasn't going to let him get under my skin. I didn't want to run the risk of getting binned over the issue.

I took all he could throw at me for a few weeks, but gradually he managed to get through my defenses.

The straw that broke the camel's back was during one of his infamous locker inspections. He was in a particularly bad mood that morning and had been screaming and yelling for a while as he made his way through the accommodation block, to our room. We all knew that we were in for it and had braced ourselves for the worst, like a car skidding on black ice towards a tree. Everyone was on edge as the inevitable storm approached our room.

As he flew into our room like a miniature tornado, he made a beeline for me, bypassing several others, and hit me so hard in the chest that I flew backwards into my locker, ending up in a heap inside. Without thinking I was on my feet in an instant, standing back to attention, facing up to him, fists clenched at my side. I wanted so much to hit him right in the mouth, but only the fear of being binned held me back.

He moved so close that his nose was almost touching mine, and I could feel the heat from his face on mine. "You frightened of me, Moore?" he yelled, spittle flying from his mouth across my face. I didn't flinch. I stared him right in the eyes.

"No Staff!" I shouted back, making sure my spittle hit his face in return.

"You ******* well should be!" he prodded me again, rocking me on my feet. He was really trying to get me to react that day.

"There's only one thing scares me, Staff!"

He stepped back a few inches, and then turned around the room, pacing like a very dangerous animal. The threat of violence hung in the air like a dark cloud of oppression. Rumor had it that he had been in the French Foreign Legion during his youth. I believed it. He was a beast of a man.

"You'd better tell me then, hadn't you Moore." He had a great smirk on his face, an extremely tempting target at that point and it took an immense effort not to slam my fist into his face.

I stepped in closer to him, a flashback coming of my knife fight with Colin. My voice was very low as I spoke. "You'll bin me if I have a go at you, won't you Staff." It was a statement of fact and not a question.

He simply folded those huge, tattooed arms." Fancy your chance with me, do you Moore?"

I knew that I wouldn't stand much of a chance but I'd have a go for sure. I just met his gaze, unflinching.

Several seconds passed and then he simply grinned at me and turned to leave the room. "Sort that locker out."

I never had trouble with Staff Lamont again.

One of the great levelers of basic training was the physical training sessions everyone had to partake in, known simply as PT. Although all of us were young, average age 18 or so, not everyone was as fit as they should've been, myself included. Almost from the start PT was a dreaded and hated stage we had to go through, sometimes several different forms each day, from running to gym work, with everything from sit ups to weight lifting and circuit training.

A Physical Training Instructor (PTI) always ran the PT sessions. On the surface these men look like any other human being- but the similarities stop right there! They are a species set apart from every other person on planet earth! Fit to the point beyond the reach of most people they pushed us day after day, in and outside of the gym, to a point where pain became a constant unwelcome companion during the sessions, like teeth being pulled without the pain killers.

The PTIs were absolute fanatics about fitness and came down very hard on anyone they thought slacking and watched us like hawks. Yet looking back I can see that they were also very fair working each of us hard, building up the stamina that we needed for active duty. Even the worst of us soon became more fit and healthy than at any other time in our short lives.

It was also exciting to see how we were coming together as an intake, remembering the first few runs we did. They were a real mess in every sense of the word with most of us, including myself, unable to complete the three-mile course. Running in formation was difficult as well but we soon learnt how to, and once you'd got the hang of it, it actually helped you to cover the distances we covered.

Certain standards had to be met and soon we were meeting, then excelling at these basic requirements. It felt good. I had never been fit and found it all a huge challenge but did my best. And it was paying off.

There was one particular training run that was feared by just about every soldier on the camp. A route was taken that led up a long, long, long track up into the hills nearby. Part sand, part tarmac, part chalk it was a real killer as the slope stretched up for nearly one mile. It was a fearsome and grueling slog up the seemingly endless slope. Then after the briefest of rests, back down again and back to camp. A real killer.

On our first attempt not one of us actually made it to the top running. Walking yes, staggering yes, and running, no way! We were a pathetic sorry sight as we struggled to the highest point. Some were sick with the strain of it all, especially in the heat of the day. This was a harsh exercise and required as much mental endurance as physical to beat the hill.

Once at the top we then had to make it all the way back to the camp, sometimes straight down the hill, occasionally by a different route. The whole event left you battered and exhausted. The PTIs, of course, didn't even break sweat or get out of breath and for this we held them in even more awe.

After the first of the Chalk Hill Runs, as they were known, I went back along the route alone a few days later on my day off, determined to make it in one go. It nearly killed me but I made it, covering the last hundred yards at a very slow pace but I never stopped running once. An elderly snail could've overtaken me for the last few yards, but I made it all the same, by sheer willpower alone.

As the run was a monthly event for the entire camp of several hundred men, including all of the regular staff and all the officers, I decided that I was going to get as fit as I personally could over the next three weeks before the next official run. Most weekends and even some midweek evenings when spare I would clear off and tackle the dreadful run alone. I told no one where I was going, all the lads assuming I was on a fitness craze.

When the next run was announced at morning parade I was supremely confident that I would make it and was actually looking forward to it, having regularly made it to the top.

The afternoon of the run was one of the hottest of the summer, making things just that bit tougher. After the long run leading in to the bottom of the hill, I just reached in deep and went for it going up the hill like a racing snake and I soon found myself in the leading group as we hit it head on, much to the amazement of the PTIs. I felt sick and hurt all over my body but was filled by an incredible sense of achievement at what I had done. I had ample time to recover and watch as the others struggled up the hill.

One of the PTIs came over to me, a surprised look on his face." Well done, Moore." Was all he said and I nearly burst with pride. It wasn't often a PTI gave out praise. I had worked hard for this.

A week later we were sent off to the closest thing to hell on earth I had ever experienced in my life.

Longmore camp.

The huge training area that surrounded Longmore camp was very bleak and inhospitable to us as we made camp and put up the small tents that were to be home for the next period of our basic training. This was the time when we would be turned into soldiers capable of fighting on a battlefield against the enemy. Although our job was to be Army policemen we were, first and foremost, soldiers able to fight.

The time at Longmore was designed to weed out the unsuitable and was rumored to be very nasty indeed. I had spoken to other lads further along in the training than us who had completed Longmore, and what they had told me, even allowing for the usual exaggeration, wasn't very nice.

But the greatest incentive of all was that if we passed Longmore, then we would be allowed to wear the coveted Red Cap of the RMP and then begin the law school segment.

The first day at Longmore was very nearly the last for many of us.

As a squad we were run out to a large sandy clearing near our tents, with trees on three sides. Lying on the ground, as if dropped from the heavens, were four brown wooden telegraph poles about twenty-five feet long. I wondered what they were doing there.

The training staff stood near the poles, some of them grinning at us with a superior look, knowing something that we didn't. As I looked at those poles a sudden sense of foreboding filled me as I realized just what those poles were for, remembering a conversation from someone back at RMPTC.

An NCO stepped forward. "I want 8 men on each of these poles. GO!" he yelled at the top of his considerable voice. We rushed forward and there were a few minutes of utter confusion as we sorted ourselves out. He gave the next command.

"On the word LIFT, you will lift the pole and place it on your shoulders. HAVE YOU GOT IT?"

"YES STAFF."

Again there were the smiles from those watching us.

"LIFT."

We hefted the heavy poles up onto our shoulders, the weight not too bad at that point. That would soon change and I could already feel the bite of the wood on my skin.

The NCO simply turned, shouting over his shoulder, "FOLLOW ME." He then began to jog away. So we followed and began, what is known to soldiers around the world, as the Log Run. The exercise is designed to get a group of soldiers to work together as a team. Basic and very crude, but it always works without fail.

On an even surface it is possible to manage reasonably well as long as everyone keeps working together, but it was when we hit the sandy slopes and muddy tracks that filled the training area that the Log Run became the severest test any of us had ever faced in our lives. It was sheer murder.

The next hour was awful and when we arrived back at the start point, moving at a snail's pace, gasping and wheezing like a geriatrics day out, we were given a little pep talk from the NCO leading us on the run.

"That was the easy route today," again that sadistic smile filled his face," Just to break you guys in and to let you know what you are facing."

I think that all of us were shocked and awed at the word 'Easy route.'

"We will be using the logs EVERYDAY that you are our guests here at Longmore camp. If you can work as a team, then you will make it. If not...." He let the words hang in the air. He was true to his word and took us out every single day, longer and faster, even tackling obstacles such as rivers and crossing ditches. But he was right as it built up teamwork to a point I'd never believed possible.

A vital part of our training was the use of weapons and we spent many hours on the firing ranges nearby, learning to fire and operate a variety of weapons, from pistols to sub machine guns. Before leaving for Longmore there had been intensive lectures and practical sessions on the weapons we would be using, so the basics were in place when we arrived. Hundreds of rounds were fired at paper targets at the bottom of the range. In the lulls between shooting, most of us took the chance to simply lie down on the ground and sleep for a few precious minutes. I had never been so tired in all my life. Once again my time in the Air Cadets came in handy, as I had been used to firing rifles, gaining the coveted RAF marksman badge. We were also tested on clearing stoppages and various problems a weapon can have. It was hard but very enjoyable when things went well.

Hours were spent out in the open learning the art of how to camouflage ourselves from any enemy looking for us. I had a bad time with blisters on my hands as we had to dig deep trenches in the hard packed ground, and then conceal them. The staff taught us how to slither across open ground without being seen, using the ground to its best advantage. We were looking and acting like soldiers now.

It was tough and tiring and we had, on average, about two hours sleep in any twenty-four hour period. We were being pushed and pulled beyond our limits as the staff tried to break us and make us cave in. For each and every one of us it was a personal battle, physically, mentally, emotionally, just to keep going and make it through one more day. But as the team spirit developed and blossomed we drew strength from each other. Our world had shrunk to the confines of the training ground and the day at hand. Nothing else mattered except making it through the day.

Another big challenge was keeping clean whilst living out in the field, most importantly our weapons.

The staff would carry out spot checks to see if we had been cleaning and oiling our guns, the idea being that they would be in top condition and ready to fire at any time. A dirty weapon could jam when needed most and could cost lives.

Staff Lamont, of all people, caught me out once for having a dirty weapon. Some mud had dried inside the barrel. I received a royal screaming at from him. "Your life and others depend on this weapon, Moore!" he waved the weapon around like a sword and I thought I was going to get hit with it. I even ducked as he let rip.

"Won't happen again, Staff." I assured him, knowing I was completely in the wrong in this.

"If it does, then you're out!" he jabbed me in the chest to make the point. "Understood?"

I nodded, understanding all too well. From that point on whenever we stopped or had a break of any length, I would pull the cleaning rag through the barrel, giving it a light coating of oil. I became very adept at stripping down my SMG within seconds, then assembling it once again just as fast. I even managed to impress the staff with this. I learned to do it blindfolded as if doing it in the dark. No way was I going to give Staff Lamont the chance to see me binned from the course for a dirty weapon. I had learned my lesson.

And as sure as night follows day, Lamont grabbed me a few days later, right after a Log Run and checked my weapon. No one else, only me. It was impeccably clean and ready for use. Again he gave me one of his evil-looking grins. Looking back now I actually think that he was on my side, just pushing me that little bit harder than anyone else.

The days and nights passed in a blur of sleepless nights and long, hard days that never seemed to end, merging into a seamless rock face of pain. It was a steep learning curve for all of us. But for all that I enjoyed it all.

The course at Longmore culminated with a day/night exercise putting into practice all that we had learned during our time here. It was, without doubt, the greatest challenge any of us had ever faced in our short lives as we listened to the plan of action for the exercise. We had also been left in no doubt that if we failed this then we would be binned, kicked out of the RMP. The tasks we had been set were just about impossible to complete. Or so we thought at the time. It's amazing what you can do if your heart is in something.

We had come through too much to fail now, in that we were all decided. So we slogged it out, giving it everything that we had, every man pulling his weight.

At roll call at Ex-End, the training staff gathered before us, stony faced, giving nothing away at all. None of us knew if we had passed. We were all so tired it was difficult to even stand up straight. I was seeing double and felt wasted.

Staff Lamont called out the names of all those who had passed. When my name came, he looked over at me and nodded. Then he smiled, a real first, and I returned the smile. I had made it through Longmore.

Back at the RPMTC after a short ceremony, we were presented with our bright red berets and allowed to wear them for the first time. I wore mine with pride.

I was well on the way to finishing the course and becoming a fully-fledged Royal Military Policeman.

One of the perks of completing the Longmore course was that we were all given a long weekend pass and so I headed back to Thetford by train. I wore my uniform with pride and enjoyed the looks I was getting, especially from the girls as I swaggered along practicing my tough look.

On arrival home Mum and Bob were pleased to see me and we got on like a house on fire. I even took Bob out for a drink at a local pub, knocking back the pints like real pro, telling huge stories that got bigger by the hour.

On Saturday I took a slow walk through the Thetford shopping precinct, again in uniform, soaking up the glances I was getting from people as I passed them by. This was where I had decided to become a soldier.

I even nodded to a young lad standing by the exact same brick wall I had.

Strange or what!

The next and perhaps most important hurdle for me to clear was the intensive Basic Military Law course that had to be passed and with good results. Since it was the RMP's role to enforce military law anywhere the British Army served we had to be very proficient and knowledgeable on everything from the current Theft and Assault laws, right through to the Road Traffic Act, down to the Code of Military Conduct on behavior and dress code. It wasn't just head knowledge that was needed but the ability to translate it into the practical.

The weeks spent in lectures and classroom learning all this was a massive and sometimes insurmountable challenge to me and my lack of schooling very soon began to show as I really struggled to keep up with the course work. Others seem to fly through every lecture, able to memorize all that was required. I was getting behind and in serious trouble and I didn't know what to do about it.

One saving grace during this time was Driving School. Since every RMP had to be able to drive whilst on duty it was down to the Army to get us a license and so halfway through Law School I was enrolled onto the two week intensive driving course. The RMP even has its own instructors for this purpose. For the next couple of weeks I did nothing but drive around in and around the South coast of England, enjoying the summer days. It was also a very necessary break for me.

My civilian-driving instructor, who name is long gone from memory, was a very quiet, taciturn man whose only words to me each, apart from Good Morning and Goodbye, were to give me directions as we covered the miles. Apart from this he was silent. This, to be honest, really got on my nerves and one day as we took a tea break at a roadside cafe. I challenged him about why he didn't talk to me. I had begun to take it personally and thought that somehow I'd offended him in some way.

His explanation was really very simple. "Gary," he said as he sipped his mug of tea, "Next week when you take your test the examiner will say even less that I do. Get used to it now and you will fly through the actual test."

It all now made sense. I felt a little silly for asking. The matter sorted I got down to the job in hand, learning to drive in the long wheel base Land rover which was a bit of a beast to handle as it had no power steering or assisted brakes. But it was standard issue throughout the British Army.

One amusing incident was the day we went to Bogor Regis, a small seaside town on the coast. Up until I saw the signpost I'd thought that it was a place that people made up, as it had been the butt of many jokes on the TV. To prove that I'd been there I sent my Mum a postcard. It was a lovely place.

A week later I took my test, failing the first time due to a minor accident on the road. A few days later I made no mistake and passed with flying colors, gaining my driver's license.

After a few days leave following driving school it was back to the

dreaded classrooms and hours of lectures. I was really struggling by this point and as much as others tried to help me with my studies this was something that had to be completed alone. After all the team effort of Longmore Camp
I suddenly felt totally out of my depth and very alone. The prospect of the coming examinations scared me, as I knew I would fail. And if I failed, then I was out. As simple as that.

Help, however, was at hand in the unlikely form of Sergeant Jeff Kendall. Compared to the other tutors he was a fun person who made the lessons come alive and, more to the point, easy to remember. I looked forward to his teaching.

Somehow he wrangled it so that he could take over nearly all of the course work for our intake, which was fine by me. He was due to retire from the Army in a few short weeks and was keen to pass on to us 22 years of experience as a RMP.

Under Sgt Kendall's tutelage I began to see what was what and quickly caught up. He suggested that when we had to learn definitions of offences that we tackled them much the same, as we would to learn a favorite poem or a song.

I gave it a try and much to my surprise it worked and well at that. For example, the definition of Assault is,

*"Assault is the intentional application of force, to the
Person of another, through act or gesture, if the person
Threatening has, or causes the person threatened, to
Believe he has the present ability to effect his purpose."*
Or the definition of Theft, is,
*"A person is guilty of theft if he dishonestly appropriates
Property, belonging to another, with the intention of
Permanently depriving the other of it. Thief and steal
Shall be construed accordingly."*

Just using this simple system enabled me to forge ahead and as exam time approached I was confident that I would pass. When the results came through my grades were not high but good enough for me to pass the course. This for me was perhaps the biggest achievement, as I had never been academically gifted.

The last and final part of training was the practical side of being an RMP and that was how to investigate minor criminal offences, or dealing with a traffic accident, taking statements and so on. I took to it all like a duck to water and was really quite happy, finally discovering, or so I thought, my purpose in this life.

The course formally ended with the Passing out Parade, full of show and pomp with a military band playing as we marched before a large crowd of friends and family. We looked wonderful that day, dressed in our

Number One uniforms, Red Caps proudly on display and newly promoted to Lance corporals.

It seemed as though our whole lives were stretching out before us and I had never been so excited and infused with life, as I was that day. After the parade we met for the last time as an intake in the large social club and we were told where in the world we were going to be posted.

As names and postings were read out there was a loud cheer after each one. I was thrilled to hear that I was going to Germany, to join 114 Provost Company, RMP.

The rest of the night was lost as we hit the booze in one big celebration.

CHAPTER EIGHT

I arrived in Germany late at night in the middle of a thunderstorm, ears still clogged up from my first ever commercial flight. Many of my mates from RMPTC were with me as we waited for someone to pick us up. The military airport at RAF Gutterslough was full and bustling and all rather confusing but I heard my name called out by a RMP soldier in camouflage gear and, after quick handshakes all round, I was off heading through the driving rain to the waiting MP land rover, my transport to my first posting.

My opening few days on joining 114 Provost Company RMP in Minden, West Germany, was a blur of events, faces and things to do. I was the only one posted to Minden from my course and felt very alone in those initial few days as I settled in.

As RMP we had our own two stories building as living accommodation exclusively for us to use. Traditionally the RMP is segregated from other Army units for two reasons as a general rule.

One is that Military Policemen always have to be impartial in the administration of justice to the soldiers they have to police. It's very hard to investigate a friend. As I was told more than once: familiarity breeds contempt.

Secondly, and maybe more importantly, most soldiers hate RMP's and wouldn't take too kindly to sharing accommodation with them. At this time I was blissfully unaware of this and really was an innocent abroad. This was soon to change.

My room was shared with two other lads themselves recent arrivals in the last few months but they were already old hands and they quickly filled me in on what was what. The whole time was a very steep learning curve for me but that was the way things were and you got on with it. It felt good to be accepted and I was as keen as mustard to learn everything that I could and asked endless questions of my roommates.

I soon found out that other army units didn't like us too much by the looks that some of them gave me as I walked around Kingsley barracks, our home base, dressed smartly and wearing my red beret with enormous pride, trying to find out where everything was. I soon realized that being friendly was definitely not on and after a few days I adopted a rather fearsome scowl whenever I walked around the camp.

The segregation extended even to the mess hall where a tall wooden partition blocked us off from the rest of the hundreds of soldiers eating there. We still had to queue up as normal but that was it. It was weird feeling at first but I soon got used to it after a few days, although I have to admit I felt awkward about being set apart.

The one bonus, however, to having our own living quarters was that we had our own social barroom right at the very top of the building, managed by one of the guys who was placed on light duties so he could keep the bar running smoothly. This was great as you could usually get a drink or a bite to eat at any time of the day or night and you didn't have too far too stumble when you were drunk!

It was a 114 Provo company tradition to get a newcomer absolutely drunk within the first few days of arrival and I was no exception as the whole unit turned up at the mess for the grand occasion. I can remember the start of the night as I was introduced to everyone but after that, well, it's just a blur!

It was a good night- I think!

My first day duty shift arrived very fast after three days of settling in and as I turned out for morning inspection I was drill parade smart, as shiny as I knew how to be. I felt almost sick with worry and nerves plus, to be honest, I still had a bit of a hangover! This was the beginning of a new way of life and I really didn't have much of a clue as to what was going to happen even though the other guys had filled me in as best they could.

After being inspected by the section sergeant, Sergeant Needham, I was taken into and introduced to, the holy of holies; the Royal Military Police Duty Room. This is the very heart of all RMP operations and is where all new arrivals learn the art of being a policeman. A very basic time but greatly needed.

A long, highly polished wooden desk filled one side of the room beneath a sliding glass window through which the public and military came for initial contact for everything from parking tickets to reporting serious crime. You never knew what was coming in next through the doors and a single swivel chair provided meagre comfort for the duty operator to meet these enquires. A safe was at the back of the room, behind the duty sergeant's desk, and contained the firearms and ammunition used by the mobile patrols. The IRA was still very active then.

A bank of constantly ringing telephones sat to one side of the window but right in the very middle of the desk was the Duty Log Book into which every telephone call, every enquiry, every coming and going of the mobile patrols out dealing with situations, were recorded in the neatest handwriting known to mankind. The log was read on a regular basis by the commanding officer and, worst of all, the company sergeant major, and was treated with an almost religious reverence, as I was later to find out to my great cost! I came to fear that book in a way I hadn't been frightened of anything before.

The first part of becoming a fully trained and operational RMP is to learn how to run the Duty Desk and this is one of the many hurdles that you have to face before you are allowed out on a mobile patrol. As the most junior and shiny Lance Corporal around and the lowest form of life that there is, it's standard practice that for the first few weeks of day and night shifts to be glued to the desk, watching and learning and dealing with the unknown. The nuts and bolts of the job. I found out later that when someone newer than I turned up then I would be released to get out on patrol more and be involved in investigations.

As the workings of the duty room were shown to me there was only one aspect that I was really unhappy with and that was something for which most people wouldn't think twice about, but for me it was a major hurdle.

Answering the telephones.

The bank of telephones seemed to be constantly ringing and therefore had to be constantly answered. At home if someone calls you think nothing of picking it up and simply saying to the caller,' hello?'

But here, in the RMP duty room, the nerve center of law enforcement in the area, it was a vastly different and precise procedure and I could see right from the start that it was going to cause me more than a few problems. You see, when I get nervous or have to speak to people I don't know too well, I begin to stutter and fall over my words. It's a secret thing that for most of my everyday life no one notices or cares about.

But here, in the Duty Room, being watched and listened to and scrutinized as I learned the basics, I knew that I was in for a hard ride. Quite frankly, I was terrified!

Even as I looked at the phones I could feel my mouth dry up and stick shut!

After a brief instruction on what to say when the phones rang, Sgt Needham motioned for the lad who sat at the desk to move away. Then he patted the chair at the desk.

"Take a seat, young Moore and let's see how you do."

I felt in that moment as if a sentence of death had been announced on me but I did as told and took the famous 'hot seat', as it was known long before 'who wants to be a millionaire' was even dreamed of.

I was acutely aware of others in the duty room as they prepared to go out on patrol and various other duties. I sat there staring at what had become a very dangerous and deadly enemy: the telephones!

I suddenly had what I considered to be a stroke of genius. I asked Sgt Needham if I could write down what I was supposed to say on answering the phone, like a script, so I could get it right. He seemed impressed by this act of initiative and dictated word for word what I had to say.

No sooner had I finished writing the last word that the unthinkable happened- a call!

Terror rose in me at that sound and I froze, hand halfway across the desk to pick up one of the receivers. I took a deep desperate breath, picked up the phone and rattled off the words I'd written down.

"Good morning114 Provo Company RMP Lance Corporal Moore speaking how can I help you?"

(If you read the above sentence as fast as you can without taking a breath then you'll have a good idea of how it sounded that day).

And that was my first baby step as a Royal Military Policeman.

As the weeks passed swiftly by I settled in very nicely indeed into the job and I found that I enjoyed the challenge of it all. Most of all I loved going out on mobile patrol in the RMP land rovers through the streets of Minden, watching out for drunken British soldiers or dealing with Road Traffic Accidents involving service people. I was also involved in a few minor investigations concerning thefts from a local army barracks. It was impossible to know what was going to happen next when the radio called. Best of all I got a big kick out of being fully armed with a loaded nine-millimeter pistol. Looking back it was like giving a child a gun to play with as apart from basic training back at Chichester on a firing range shooting at paper targets I really wonder what would've happened if we had of been involved in a shootout! I shudder to think.

I still remember one particular day when we got a radio call to attend a bad accident on the outskirts of Minden. I was driving that day familiarizing myself with the streets and routes and so I turned on the blue flashing emergency lights on the roof and hit the button for the loud sirens as we sped to the scene of the crash.

This was my very first 'blue light run' that I had actually driven on and I was enjoying every second of it all, twisting and turning through the heavy traffic, overtaking along the central white lines in the broad German roads. What adrenalin buzz it was.

The accident wasn't too bad with no one hurt except for the damaged vehicles and after taking details we resumed the roving patrol, eagerly awaiting the next shout. The only call we got was to return to base.

On arrival Staff Sergeant Redfurn met us in the car park. Staff Redfurn was a short, rotund man who was always impeccably turned out. His gruff Yorkshire accent and weathered face made him look like a grizzled bulldog.

"I understand you've just had your first blue light run, Moore."

I nodded," Yes Staff."

"Any problems?" he asked in a tone I should've picked up on.

"No." I pulled out my notebook and began to explain in detail about the accident we had attended, feeling very pleased with myself that I had recorded all the facts as taught back at the RMPRC.

"Well that's fine," there was a pause as Staff Redfurn took a deep breath," but what about the cars that YOU hit as you drove like a *******idiot to the scene?" his face had turned a bright red, a sight I was to see often as he got angry at someone or something. It was usually me.

I just stood there looking blank, lost for words. Hit cars? I had no idea what he was on about.

He jabbed me in the chest," You hit two parked cars, scraped a third as you overtook and narrowly missed killing a pedestrian on a crossing!" his voice hit me like a powerful jet of water. "And all you can do is stand there looking like an idiot. GET OUT OF MY SIGHT!"

I quickly left the lion's den and retreated back into the relative safety of the duty room. The rest of the section were there waiting for me. I was greeted with grins and laughter at my obvious discomfort after the tongue-lashing I had just received.

One of the guys, Luigi, grinned and said, "Welcome to the club!"

I later found out that most, if not all, managed to hit something at some stage on blue lights runs. However, I did manage to hold the dubious distinction of causing the most damage on a first run for quite some time.

As I mentioned before we had our own bar in our living block and before long I was soon drinking heavily as I became immersed in the culture of the RMP. The combination of segregation and easy access was a breeding ground for drinking problems.

I had always enjoyed a drink like most young men of my age, but the availability night and day was making it too easy for me. I noticed within days of arrival that many lads seemed permanently tanked up or had bad hangovers. I could understand why now.

Everybody drank and pushed it hard, especially the single lads and so I jumped in with both feet and was soon part of the furniture at the bar.

Little did I know it but already I was on a pathway that was leading to big trouble and to the very brink of death.

There are a number of events and incidents that took place in my first few months in Germany and one of the best was the day that I arrested a very high ranking for drunk driving.

I was out on mobile patrol in a RMP land rover by myself because it was holiday season and we also had a large area to cover. I loved being alone. I got a radio message of a traffic accident not far from the British Military Hospital at Rinteln. I blue lighted it all the way there, previous accidents forgotten about as I hurtled along. At the scene I found that an army land rover had hit a German civilian car.

The GCP (German Civil Police) had been dealing with the event but when I turned up I had authority since it was a British Army officer involved. He seemed pleased to see me.

I recognized the officer right away. He was the Deputy Provost Marshall for the whole of the British Army of the Rhine (BAOR) and was the highest-ranking officer I had ever seen, let alone met. He was in charge of all RMP operations and was very high up the command chain for the whole of Germany. I had a very big fish in my net.

I was a bit in awe of him as I took down his details and heard his side of what had taken place at the accident. I decided that I had better go right by the book and stick to the very letter of the law as I had a feeling that he would watch my every move. This was my chance to prove that I was a good RMP. I was already deciding how I would tell the story back in the bar at Minden.

At the time we had a policy of breath testing all drivers at the scene of an accident so I pulled out the test kit and asked the Officer to blow into the bag.

"Do you know who I am, young man?" was his immediate and surprised reply.

I nodded, "Yes sir, I do. But I still require you to blow into the Breathalyzer bag. Standard Operating procedure, Sir."

"Well I am not going to blow in that bag!"

"I have to inform you, Sir, that failure to blow into the bag will result in your arrest." I was playing the part beautifully and I hoped that he would be impressed by my attention to detail.

"Arrest me?" he now looked incredulous and I began to realize something was wrong. Maybe he was hoping that I would simply let him off? I nodded and held out the tube once again. He shook his head. "I will not."

And that was that.

"Sir, I am arresting you for failure to give a breath test at the scene of an accident." I then cautioned him, going right by the book and reading from my Police notebook. I was following procedure to the letter.

I then drove the Officer and myself to the Military hospital both to have him checked out but also, since he'd failed to provide a breath test, I now needed to give him the chance to give a urine sample, the next step along the way. This he also refused to give.

I rang the duty room back in Minden and explained all that was taking place. The fuse had now been lit and the fireworks were about to begin!

The duty room informed the duty sergeant who in turn informed the duty officer who hurriedly rang the detachment commanding officer who then quickly called the big boss at RMP Detmold which was the main hub for all RMP detachments like Minden.

Within minutes I was summoned to the phone at the hospital and had my first words with the commanding officer. I explained exactly what had taken place and read straight from my notebook, which I had been trained to fill in as events took place. This then became the basis for any investigation. I honestly thought that the C.O. would be pleased with me for getting things right.

But how wrong I was as the 'old boys' network swung into action.

To cut a long story short the Officer was never prosecuted and I got into trouble for being persistent in doing my job. There was, I found out the hard way, a rule for the officers and there was a rule for everyone else.

If he had simply been an enlisted soldier he would have been in deep trouble. Fined, possibly imprisoned would've been the likely outcome of such a clear violation.

The whole episode gained me enormous respect from the rest of the lads for standing my ground. News of my exploits reached far and wide. It did nothing, however, to increase my respect for the officers of the Corps.

One side effect of it all was that I became deeply disillusioned with the entire system of military justice and even began to let ordinary soldiers off with just a hard warning.

I also began to drink more than usual and adopted the attitude of some of the others and not give a damn.

><>

One of the better events was when I bought my first car, a bright yellow VW Beetle that was old when I got my hands on it. It had served a long and hard life with the German post office until it was of no further use. But to me it was as good as gold.

The windscreen wipers were hand operated and the beetle operated on 6volts, a source of huge surprise to all who saw her, and I couldn't even fit a normal radio/cassette played to her. We circumnavigated this problem by wedging in a spare car battery from a land rover behind the front seat and running a wire to the cassette player. Add some speakers and I had tunes on the move! Sorted!

The guys and me travelled many, many miles in the beetle, or the Slug, as she was affectionately known as, including one action packed trip to Amsterdam.

Eventually the Slug began to die, losing forth gear, then third gear. She was worn out and so, one night after a heavy drinking session up in the bar, we decided to give her a proper Vikings funeral.

On the spur of the moment we decided to push her to some old waste ground at the back of Kingsley barracks and set her on fire. It was a grand gesture and a great send off for a good old car.

Big trouble followed with the entire camp shut down as the slug exploded. But it had been a heap of fun and I didn't give a fig what others thought of it all. The rot had set in.

><>

As well as policing the British Army another facet of RMP work was and is to go on exercise with the main units such as tank regiments and infantry, providing a rather unique service that dates back to the world wars; route marking.

This involves placing handmade signs up at certain points directing vehicle traffic to set points thus freeing up tanks from the hassle of trying to read a map from a rocking and rolling sixty ton vehicle. Route signing could be an immensely fun job as it involved charging through the West

German countryside at high speeds and all quite legal. I loved it, as it was a boy racers dream. A lot rested on the routes being signed correctly and in good time so certain things were overlooked, unless something went wrong.

Another RMP role was to man checkpoints and to provide security for command posts from attack by enemy agents. One of the least liked duties was directing vehicles into laager points, especially at night. The worst vehicles were the huge sixty-ton chieftain tanks as you simply walked right in front of these metal monsters holding a small red-lit torch, which the tank driver was supposed to follow. It was scary stuff and you hoped that a member of the RMP had never upset a driver or you could end up in very deep trouble. I actually used to take off my red beret and hide my red and black MP armband in the hope that the drivers might just think I was an ordinary soldier. I did it both day and night just to be safe!

On one particular exercise in the depth of winter a soldier was run over and crushed to death as he guided a tank in. It's thought that he slipped and was unable to move away in time. A bad way to die.

As we were part of 4 Armored Division we were often out on some exercise or another preparing for war with the Russians who were only a few miles away in what was then East Germany. Tensions were high during the Cold War, as it was known, and many times as we were crashed out on a sudden exercise and we were never completely sure it wasn't for real.

If ever there had been a real shooting match 4 armored division was right on the very front lines and were only to hold up the advancing Russian Army long enough for the rest of B.A.O.R. to be mobilized. It was a sobering thought that life expectancy was measured in hours in the event of war. If nuclear weapons were used, then down to minutes.

My first winter in Germany was a bad one as though it had been specially ordered just for me. Driving snow one second, then came hard nasty rain and sleet slicing in on the edge of a cutting wind all the way from Siberia.

The exercise was due to last ten days but as the casualties mounted from the extreme cold the whole exercise came to a grinding halt. It was one thing to fight in such conditions but yet another to risk death during peacetime. For once one of the officers high up got things right as they announced EndEx. Those units who could make it back to base did while those further out simply battened down and waited out the bad weather. It was still a nasty experience for all involved including many old hands at winter survival.

I very nearly became one of the victims as I came to within a hairbreadth of freezing to death. We were manning a checkpoint in the middle of nowhere and over the course of the days living outside I had become wet through and not been able to dry off or change into dry kit. We had been constantly on the move trying to help out as the exercise deteriorated rapidly. I went unnoticed by our small team as we were all in the same boat, shivering and drinking warm tea to keep going. I hadn't felt my feet for days and was shivering all the time.

Because of the closeness to the West/East border it was standard operating procedure to have a guard posted at all times. I had argued against this, believing it to be rather silly but the team commander, a guy a year older than me and recently promoted to full corporal, insisted on it and I was ordered out on guard stag. The weather had cleared a little as I stepped out of the large tented area attached to our vehicle and used as our command post but the temperature was way below freezing. It was a beautiful night with a huge clear sky full of stars and my breath bloomed out in front of me like a dragon's fire and the snow cracked under foot as I slowly walked about. We had adopted a two-hour on/two hour off routine for the four of us in our section with one on radio watch and the other outside on patrol.

As the time dragged by I had to fight against a terribly compelling urge to lie down in the snow and to fall asleep, just for a few minutes. I had never known such tiredness in all my life as that time, like a quicksand holding me by the ankles. I then started having flashbacks to the time we had lost my baby brother Darren in the snow as a child and how peaceful he had been when we had finally found him.

The command tent was only about ten meters away but the thought of trying to walk across was beyond me. I was exhausted and inexorably heading into the jaws of hypothermia and certain death. I knew it was happening but the strangest thing was that I didn't have much will to do anything. Like simply falling asleep at bedtime, eyes heavy.

The only thing that I can remember was being very, very sad at the unfairness of it all. I shouldn't have even been outside and it was just the sheer bloody mindedness of the senior corporal that had placed me here. Once again in life someone else was pulling the strings.

I was vaguely aware that a land rover had pulled up right next to the command post. I'd never even heard it drive up and they were really loud as a rule. I was rooted to the spot and at the point of simply falling over.

I saw Staff Redfurn get out and on seeing me standing there like a frozen tree, bundled me inside the relative warmth of the post, shouting to wake the others up inside. They had all fallen asleep and I was outside, alone and forgotten. Without a doubt Staff Redfurn saved my life that night.

I shall never forget the pain over the following days as feeling returned to my hands and feet and I was quite ill for a while after this event. But one side effect that has lasted until this present day is that I no longer really feel the cold!

On another exercise, this time in the heat of summer my ability to think on my feet got me out of some serious trouble. In any army in any country around the planet one of the biggest crimes a soldier can commit is to be asleep on guard duty. During times of war it is an offence that carries the death penalty because of the consequences of a sentry being asleep can have such a serious effect on all those he's supposed to be guarding. If an enemy attacks then the whole camp can be taken out without warning.

On exercise Main brace we had been on the go for eight days solid with no more than a few catnaps here and there to keep us going, we were all exhausted as young and as fit as we were.

During a lull as the next phase of the exercise kicked in my detachment were given a nights rest and so we pitched tents and settled in for some food and cleaning of kit.

We all had a good meal served up by a nearby field kitchen and morale was good as the end of the exercise was in sight. As I have said before it's standard to post guard and I drew the 1am – 2am slot which was no problem to me as I could sleep before and after my stag.

The system was that the person on stag duty would wake his replacement five minutes before his turn and so on throughout the night until stand to in the morning. It was a tried and trusted method and worked well most of the time.

About 9pm I crawled into my 'green maggot', Army slang for issue sleeping bag and promptly went into a deep and comfortable sleep, ready to be kicked awake about 12.50am, ten minutes before I was due on guard.

However, the call never came and I slept through until 5.30am when all hell broke loose in the camp.

The Company Sergeant Major (CSM) had come over to our detachment for a snap visit and had found the entire camp snoring and fast asleep, snoozing in innocence and wide open to anything and anybody.

He went ballistic and shouts and yells and curses turned the early morning air blue as we all scrambled out of sleeping bags and onto parade, yawning and rubbing our eyes at the abrupt start to the day.

The CSM was in full flood and in a violently filthy mood and was out for the flesh of whoever should've been on guard. The repercussions of what had taken place were enormous and an immediate enquiry took place right there in the open air.

And it was soon discovered that the person after I was supposed to have been on after had never been woken up then the finger of suspicion soon pointed firmly in my direction, even though I pleaded that I had never been woken up either. I thought for a split second that the CSM was going to strike me as he confronted me, such was his fury. Instead he placed me under open arrest and stormed away like a tornado leaving behind a swathe of devastation.

Things were tense over the next few days before the exercise ended and I was given every dirty and filthy job going. The worst of it all for me was that for once I was innocent of anything! The guy before me, the same corporal who'd ordered me outside during the winter storm, hadn't woken me up. He had received a severe dressing down for that incident at winter and had hated me since that time. Payback time as far as he was concerned and I suspected that he had left me asleep on purpose to extract revenge. So far it was working well.

He claimed that he had woken me up, even seen me drinking a cup of tea! He was lying through his teeth and most of my mates knew it but nothing could be done for me.

I was in serious trouble.

A week after returning to base the Day of Judgment arrived for me and I was marched in before the commanding officer at Headquarters (HQ) in Detmold in double quick time to be charged with the offence of sleeping on duty, dereliction of duty.

A statement had been prepared by the corporal who had lied about waking me up and was read out to the court. It all seemed cut and dried and was very obvious that it was assumed that I was guilty. I had long since discovered that once someone's mind was made up, no matter the truth, you stood condemned.

The C.O. made various comments about my behavior, including my arrest of the senior officer for drunk driving and I have the strongest feeling that this whole issue was being pursued so very hard because of my stand in that matter as it had no bearing on what I was being charged with.

"Have you anything to say for yourself, Lance Corporal Moore, before we pass sentence?" he even glanced at his watch to show his disdain at the whole event. Typical officer. Probably thinking about what he was going to have for his lunch.

"As a matter of fact I have a couple of things to say." I took a deep breath hoping my stutter wouldn't kick in." If I was up and awake, as corporal Jones says and even drinking a cup of tea, why was I found fast asleep later on. If I was up then surely I would've woken up the next man on the list".

I looked at the faces before me to see if common sense would prevail.

I was to be disappointed and suddenly felt trapped and vulnerable with no way out of this mess.

Then in a flash I had an idea and I spoke it out without thinking. "Are you sure that I was supposed to be on at that particular time? I'm actually very positive it was supposed to be much later on than that time. I think the 4am to 5am slot." And here I played my ace-in-the-hole card. "Is there any chance that I can see the written duty roster for that night?" I tried to look innocent, as I knew full well that there wasn't such a thing and that the whole duty had been done by word of mouth.

The look on the C.O.'s face was a picture as he glanced at the R.S.M. (Regimental Sergeant Major), who quickly turned to the C.S.M. who looked very blank.

"Is there a written duty roster as evidence?" RSM asked.

"I'll check, sir." The CSM disappeared out of the room to investigate and I was taken back outside to await my fate.

I wondered how they were going to deal with this as I knew there was no written roster and to charge me then they had to prove that it was me who was supposed to be on duty, a fact that they were to trying hard to ignore and deal with me quickly. If they couldn't prove it then the whole thing should be dropped.

The C.S.M.'s face was like thunder as he stormed past me and back into the CO's office and the waiting jury, giving me a withering look as he did. He'd never liked me and I knew my cards were marked for all time now because of this, no matter the outcome.

Minutes later I was marched back inside to face the music.

"It seems that there is NO roster." The words seemed to have trouble getting out of the CO's mouth. His face was red with anger. "Did you know this, Moore? Are you trying one on with me here?" his voice was anger-packed and I knew in that instant that I had won.

I lied beautifully, "I thought that there was one, Sir, since its common practice to keep a good working record of rosters."
I tried to keep a smirk from my face and voice. I hadn't done anything wrong and now the tables were turning on the man who had accused me.

"Since I can't prove or disprove your duty time, I've no choice but to let you off with a written caution." He paused staring at me, then turned to the RSM, "Get this man out of my sight!"

As I was marched out I'm afraid the smirk broke through as I passed the corporal who had accused me, now waiting to see the CO. I gave him a long hard stare and he couldn't hold the look. He knew he had been found out and was in for it.

I'll see you later, I thought to myself, already beginning to plan revenge on this man for what he had tried to do to me by setting me up.

One of the guys had recently become a Christian and had been the butt of several jokes in the mess. Events turned serious when he announced that he wouldn't carry a weapon out on patrol, a situation that had serious implications for the section as a whole. The IRA had been very active and a few weeks back an army colonel had been assassinated outside his own home just a few miles away from Minden. Out on patrol we were keyed up and ready for anything. To have someone not willing to pack a weapon was not on. The teasing became very nasty and I was right at the forefront of it all.

Looking back now I can see why he did this and feel bad at the way I personally treated him. It took a huge amount of courage to even admit to being a Christian in an environment like this. For all the nastiness towards him there was something about his stand that appealed to me. He seemed so sure of this Jesus that he was willing to take a massive amount of nastiness. He later discharged himself from the army.

His name was Simon and I wondered what happened to him?

It was hard to be exact about the time that I realized that I had a very serious drinking problem. It had sneaked up on me like a silent attacker and I didn't know how to defend myself.

I usually started my day with a slug of rum from the bottle next to my bed, washed out my mouth after teeth cleaning with a small bottle of Herforder Pils beer, gargling away like most folks use water. It wasn't unusual for me to get though a full bottle of Captain Morgan's rum every day and that was besides what I drank publicly in the mess with the lads. I had never known addiction before and it scared me but there was no one I could talk to.

The rest of the lads thought I was great, taking risks and always pushing the limits with senior officers, bordering on the insolent. I was permanently drunk both off and on duty.

On old year's night I was on duty and our whole section, the oldest of us a mere 20 years old, was so drunk we gave up answering any calls coming into the duty room. All the senior NCOs were at home with family celebrating a new year as was normal practice.

There had been a number of calls coming into the duty room but as the evening wore on, no one was fit enough to drive anywhere to attend incidents. It was a terrible state.

The booze was dirt cheap and available in any quantity. I was fast becoming an alcoholic at 19 years old and was spiraling out of control.

My professional life was a mess and I was forever being reprimanded, many times fined, for a variety of misdemeanors from being late on duty to being slovenly attired. My personal hygiene had also gone out of the window. I was a mess.

And after my escape from the sleeping on duty charges senior people were after my blood and took every chance to pick up on me. They were like sharks out for my blood and I was bleeding badly in the water.

I knew they were after me but by now I didn't give a damn anymore. My hopes of a better life had drained away like dirty bath water down the plughole. Any thoughts of a long-term army career vaporized.

So in a nutshell I went into self-destruct mode deciding to cause as damage as possible when I exploded.

Armageddon arrived for me in the shape of an evening's drinking at the home of one of our German interpreters, a good man called Willi Brandt.

Willi had been born in pre-war Nazi Germany in the 1920's but had moved to Australia of all places to escape the impending disaster his parents had foreseen taking place. A wise move it turned out indeed. After the war they had returned finding a devastated and divided Germany, carved up by the victors into East and West Germany. Work had been scarce but since Willi hadn't been involved in the war in anyway and had in fact served in the Australian army and spoke good English, albeit with an Aussie twang, he'd found employment as an interpreter for the British Army, eventually ending up with the RMP in Minden towards the end of his working life.
Willie was a good guy who liked his drink a little too much and was constantly harangued by his lovely wife about it all. I can't remember her name but she was like a second mother to many of us, putting on heaps of food when we turned up.

It was a lovely warm evening as a bunch of us sat outside drinking and eating, one of those occasions where nothing else mattered and all problems are left outside the front door.

Willi was regaling us with stories of his time living in the outback of Australia and of his travels to the Far East and his jungle training in the depths of Borneo.

As the booze flowed the tales got wilder with accounts of huge and deadly dangerous snakes and how he had to hack his way through miles of impenetrable jungle for weeks on end.

One of the lads remarked that he couldn't hack his way out of a wet paper bag, much to everyone's laughter. With an upset grunt Willi disappeared away and into his large house and was gone for a while. We all wondered if he had been hurt by our ribbing and several of us were on the point of going to look for him, when he suddenly returned, triumphantly holding a very long and very wicked looking jungle machete. It was obviously an extremely dangerous weapon but to me was a thing of loveliness. My breath was sucked away in an instant. I can still feel it right now.

For about ten minutes Willi waved the machete around, dangerously close to his audience as he demonstrated with vigor how he had slashed and cut and hacked his way through the thick impenetrable jungle. After a few near misses we decided that it would be safer for everyone present if he put it down for a while. I asked Willi if I could hold it and as he handed it over I felt that same old thrill of excitement rippled through me. It was a nice feeling.

At well over 16 inches long and razor sharp it was more than capable, in the right hands, of cutting off someone's arm, let alone a jungle vine. As I sat there in the gathering gloom of Willies back garden I simply savored its weight and latent violence. It was lovely.

Suddenly Willi made a loud drunken announcement to all who could hear. He was giving me the machete as a gift, a token, of our friendship. We had always got on well and he had taken me under his ruffled wings when I had first arrived.

Willi hugged me and made a great fuss of me in front of all the lads who lapped it up, clapping and cheering and demanding a speech from me, which I gladly provided from on top of the food table.

It was a fabulous evening, but once again it seemed as though I was going to get in trouble with a knife. And this time it was going to be very, very serious and have consequences that would last.

The night wore on and after leaving Willi in a drunken stupor we all headed back to the camp and carried on our drinking up in the mess which would stay open as long as we were there.

For some weeks now I had been getting slowly more and more violent when drunk and had been remarked on by many of the lads. There was a point when it was wise to just get out of my way and leave me alone. There had been one night just a few days before when I had been smashed and had stood outside on the waste ground near the camp and had yelled and screamed in sheer anger at the stars. Apparently it had been heard all over the camp.

It was just seemed that the boiling rage that had filled me for so long couldn't be contained any longer. I was on the point of exploding and someone was going to get hurt.

As we drank late into the night I vaguely remember looking around at some of the ten or men in there. Some I liked and was glad to call them mates. Others I had no opinion or one way of the other, they were just there in the background of my life.

But there was a couple there that I really detested and I was soon in a very nasty fight, which spilled out onto the stairway. Some of my closer mates pulled me off before any real damage was done. It was accepted that there would be scraps among us and a blind eye was adopted unless it was serious. This was getting close to the mark. Blood had flowed this night.

Some tried to calm me down but how do you reason with blind anger? Impossible, especially when drunk.

I left the mess and went down to my room looking for my King Edward cigars, which I had discovered recently and quite enjoyed smoking. The machete lay on top of my bed where I had thrown it on getting back from Willie. I recalled seeing the corporal, who had wrongly accused me of sleeping on duty, heading for the duty room as he was on the night shift.

A huge tsunami of anger welled up in me as I thought of that man and what he had tried to do to me. I hefted the machete in my hands and with a resolve that almost sobered me up; I headed downstairs and for the duty room.

As I yelled and shouted and stumbled downstairs some of the guys guessed where I was off too and ran ahead and warned the duty room I was heading that way. Things by this time had got very serious. I was a danger to life and limb now and everyone kept at a distance. But I didn't know all this until later as I was heading, avalanche like, to get the man who'd betrayed me.

And all I could think of was killing him. Murder was in my heart. And I was more than capable.

Unknown to me the corporal in question that I wanted to kill had been cleared out quickly by some of the guys who had warned him I was coming so when I got there I simply went ballistic because he wasn't there. I waved the machete around at those still there demanding to know where he was, and then I began to slash and hack at the duty room desk, yelling and screaming vile words, bits and chunks of the wood flying everywhere. The duty Log was slashed into bits. I smashed the glass window and then hacked at the other desks in the room. I was alone in the room doing my worst.

Because of all the IRA activity all on-duty RMP carried pistols and were fully armed. As I went berserk the duty sergeant pulled out his pistol, cocked it, and as I was told later, prepared to shoot me if I tried to attack anyone. I was an immediate and deadly danger to life at that time. The damage I was causing could be fixed but if I hit a person with that wicked blade they could be mutilated or worse.

At one point I moved towards him and dared him to shoot me dead, to finish all the hurt in my life. Today there is a term for this in America, 'death by cop', where those wanting to die actually cause the cops to shoot them.

That's where I was at that point. For some reason I didn't attack him, but left the building, screaming like a mad man, like Legion in the Bible account, rampaging in the grounds of Kingsley barracks.

I slashed at cars and trees out of control. The whole camp saw and heard me and knew I was RMP.

Somehow I made it into my room without injuring anyone, a miracle in itself, locking the door behind me and I then smashed up all that I owned. I finished off all the booze I had in the room, and then passed out on my bed.

The sword of Damocles fell very early in the morning as a snatch squad of soldiers burst in through my door, a swift and very violent entry designed to catch me off guard as I was still armed with the machete. I was manhandled off my bed, still fully clothed and covered in vomit, and pressed to the floor and handcuffed none too gently. A few kicks to my side winded me badly.

It had been decided to leave me until morning, as I would in all probability be passed out, as was the case.

I was vaguely aware of being cautioned as I was unceremoniously dragged and carried across to the main barrack's guardroom and thrown into a single prison cell. The door was slammed shut and I remember the sound as it crashed into my already painful hangover. Not a good way to start the day for sure.

As I sat there, head in hands, I realized that I was in deep trouble this time, nothing that I could explain away or talk myself out of.

Things definitely didn't look good and as I looked around my new home in the prison cell I suddenly understood that this was exactly like my entire life: empty.

><

Events moved quickly after my arrest. I spent a number of days in the prison cells and then transferred to company HQ and placed in yet another cell awaiting Courts Martial, the highest court a soldier can be sent to.

All I came across shunned me as I had disgraced the RMP big time and wasn't even spoken too and they treated me like a pariah. I had caused thousands of pounds of damage, nearly been shot and killed, and apparently chased after someone with the machete, although that I can't remember. All in all a bad nights work.

Long hours spent thinking in my prison cell went on trying to figure out just where I had gone so badly wrong, just when it seemed that I was overcoming my past problems. Truth was, I really loved being a soldier in the RMP.

Despair was an unwelcome cellmate but a very present one at that.

Finally the big day arrived.

><

The Courts Martial took less than ten minutes from its beginning to its pre-ordained end.

The charges were read out listing the details of all that had transpired that fateful night, together with the recommendations of the sentence to be handed out.

To be honest at this point I didn't really give a damn what happened to me, the hope of future sucked out of me. I hadn't seen or heard a friendly face now for weeks, just left to myself in my cell.

Eventually, more as a formality, I was asked if there was anything I wanted to say to the court. I simply shrugged my shoulders and laughed at the absurdity of it all, a big grin all over my face, showing my utter contempt of the lot of them. Not one of them had tried to help me but instead just kept bashing me with the rulebook.

The RSM went mad again and got right in my face shouting at me for my disrespect of the CO. I toyed with the idea of head butting the man. After all what more could they do to me?

I blew the RSM a kiss. "Guilty as charged." I grinned.

"You are to be stripped of your rank and dishonorably discharged from Her Majesty service. Dismissed!"

So, that was that. Demoted and soon to be kicked out. I put on a big show as I was marched back to my cell, sauntering along much to the fury of the RSM.

As he closed the door on me I smiled at him, raised my middle finger to him and had the pleasure of hearing him exploding in rage.

Events moved quickly after this and I was flown back to the RMPTC, the very place I had trained so hard to pass the course. During my time I spent there as the paperwork was sorted for my discharge a change took place in me. Hope seemed absent and I had never felt so empty in all my life. There was a constant bubbling of anger and violence under the surface that was only held in check by the thinnest of threads.

One particular incident sums up what I had become in a terrifying way.

Because of my status as waiting for discharge I was given all kinds of boring and dirty jobs to keep me occupied and hopefully out of trouble. Working in the stores counting boots and so on.

One fine day I was detailed to act as cook for the directing staff on one of the many outdoor training exercises that all new recruits go out on. I had been on this during my own time here and it was a tough period in the life of new recruits.

My job was simple enough. I had to cook three meals a day for the training staff and always have a brew of tea on at all times. It was a simple enough job and I didn't mind it as I was left alone most of the time, as they were busy giving the recruits a rough time.

However there was a very junior officer, straight out of SandHurst Military Academy who joined the course for a couple of days to see how things were done. I had never liked officers and found them arrogant and unduly nasty. This one was no exception and he took a real dislike to me when he found out that I was being dishonorably discharged and went out of his way to be nasty and rude to me.

It came to a head when I was tasked to cook a meal for three people and then the officer turned up, looked in the pot and saw that there wasn't enough for four people. He turned on me in a spiteful tirade of abusive words that even made the directing staff uncomfortable. It was uncalled for.

All he had to do was to ask me to do some more food but no, he had to be cruel.

It was then that I decided to kill him and suddenly I felt the calmest that I had done in a very, very long time. I gave the officer a cold smile and added to the pot, planning his death.

As I sat alone that evening, seething with anger, a rather splendid idea came to mind. From where I was sitting I could see the sleeping area with small two man tents set up. The officer had one to himself, of course, and was slightly removed from the others, as if to reinforce his status as our better.

Just in my line of sight was one of the petrol jerry cans that were used to fuel the cooking stoves and to top up the vehicles tanks. I decided that the easiest way to kill the officer was to pour petrol down the slight slope onto his tent, and simply set fire to it while he was in there and sleeping. A good plan I thought but how would I get away with it? That was the problem.

As dusk ebbed in I pondered the problem with a certainty that I would have answer before long.

By early evening the answer had come to me. In full view of everyone I moved several of the jerry cans away from the side of the lorry I lived and slept in and cooked from and placed the cans further away, about fifteen feet away from the officers tent. I explained it away as they were too close to the cooking area.

No one took much notice as night was drawing in and the staff were enjoying some of the sandwiches I had made along with a steaming pot of tea. I warned everyone to watch out for the cans in the dark and to be careful of smoking nearby. I was setting the scene for what was to follow.

My plan was simple. At around 4am I would get up and pour the petrol down the slope making sure that it soaked the officer's tent, then simply drop a lighted cigarette into the petrol and burn the man alive. I would run back into my sleeping quarters in the back of the lorry. Hopefully the blame would be put on the shoulders of the sentries smoking in the area who would be accused of knocking over the cans. Simple. I also had no problem with lying and saying that I saw one of the sentries smoking nearby.

A coldness filled me at the prospect of killing the officer who had wrong me yet there was also a curious excitement that was both exhilarating and frightening at one and the same time. I had in my hands the power of life and death.

It tasted very good at that point in time.

As I cleared up for the night the officer came past and didn't even acknowledge my existence. I couldn't resist a word to the condemned.

"Have a good night's sleep, sir."

He paused and was about to say something but the look on my face must have worried him as I stood there grinning. He grunted something and retired to his tent, which, as far as I was concerned, was now his grave.

><>

As I lay in the back of the lorry, wrapped against the cold in my sleeping bag I was tense and wound up. I planned to get up at about 4am and do the deed. Normally I would be woken up at 5am by one of the sentries to get breakfast ready but I was always awake by that time anyway. I set my alarm clock for 4am and finally drifted off to sleep.

><>

I do remember that my sleep was troubled, with visions of fire and screaming and somewhere I could hear my own name being shouted," *Moore, Moore, Moore.*"

I was shaken awake by the sentry to find that I had slept right through my alarm and was now 5am. Because I'd over slept a man had lived.

I started my day bitterly disappointed.

On return to base at the weeks end I was told I was going to be leaving officially on the Monday. So that what that. Once more another failure.

On Monday, as promised, I was thrown back into civilian life like an unwelcome fish back to the river.

CHAPTER NINE.

My return home to Thetford was a less than glorious affair with no brass bands playing to welcome me and certainly no banners across the metal foot bridge on the A11 road that split the town in half. The train station that morning seemed a desolate kind of place, as I was the only passenger to step off the train.

I'd called mum the night before from the RMPTC just hours after being officially Dishonorably Discharged from Her Majesty's Armed Forces. As usual I had come up with an extremely plausible excuse as to why I was leaving the Army. I distinctly remember mum not being too keen on my return home and to be honest I can't say that I blame her for that.

But I'd consoled her with the fact that it wouldn't be for too long. That bit of my lie was true anyway.

I was assigned the sofa in the front room, which wasn't too bad to sleep on, and there was space under the stairs for my gear. That was my lot as my old bedroom had been taken over by my younger brother, Darren, and sisters Debbie and Rachel were sharing. There was no room at the inn.

That first evening home was spent having a good drink with mum and Bob, as I spun the story for my discharge as having been through a traumatic incident on a training exercise and therefore was no longer fit for service. As the drink flowed my tale got more harrowing by the hour.

Bob had recently left the United States Army Air Force, or USAAF for short, after 22 years of service and I felt a real fraud lying to the man. He had completed his terms of service, with a couple of tours of Vietnam thrown in, while I had fallen in the first couple of years and had failed miserably.

As we sat and talked that night I wondered why on earth I had never got on with him before now. Strange how life works out, isn't it?

The next day I went over to Beccles, Suffolk, to see my beloved Granny and she was absolutely overjoyed to see me and, as I told her a less gruesome version of my story, I felt really dreadful at lying to her the way that I did. Trouble is once you start a lie it just burrows deeper and deeper until it's almost impossible to discern between the fact and the fiction.

However the outcome of my visit was that she asked me to move in with her, into the room I used to have as a child. Since Granddads death she had been living alone and would enjoy my company.

I accepted on the spot, grateful for the lifeline extended to me, knowing just how much I needed a break in fortune just then. I moved in a couple of days later.

The wonder of it all was that it seemed as though I had gone back in time to my childhood as Granny looked after me, cooking and making sure I was all right. There was no pressure on me, not a drop, for me to do anything or be anything. Sometimes we would simply sit in the front room and just talk or listen to the radio while Granny knitted. I was in the safest place it was possible for me to be.

On most days I would go out for long, long walks out across the common and then further out to the marshes way past the new bypass that was being built, and to the river. Sometimes I went back over events in life, trying to figure things out, to make sense of it all. Other days I would just walk, almost on autopilot, hardly remembering where I had been.

As I walked I also drank, not dreaming of doing that at Granny's. I knew my life was an absolute mess, everything that I had hoped and dreamed for of being a soldier ruined and destroyed by forces seemingly out of my control. It was as though some inner demons had power over my life and that there wasn't a single thing I could do to stop their destructive influence on my life.

I had the awful feeling that I was being sucked, dragged almost, into a deep, dark pit without a bottom and had no choice in the matter.

Despair was my constant companion as I walked those long days in solitude whatever the weather threw at me.

I knew that when I returned to 23 Common Lane that I would be safe and sound with Granny. She never asked me questions about where I had been just simply took care of me and loved me as only a grandparent can do with a grandchild. It's called unconditional love and very rare.

After three weeks my money began to run out and I decided that I needed to find a job, not just to give Granny some rent but also because I needed to fund my secret drinking, although it wasn't as bad as it had been.

The only job I could find with an immediate start was a night shift at a local factory, MeatPak, which produced all kinds of meat-based food. I took it and started on the Monday.

The pay was ok for me as a single man and I soon found that I was drinking heavily again. Once Granny quizzed me and, to my eternal shame, I lied barefaced to her, saying I was fine and didn't have a drink problem. She just smiled and advised me to stick to tap water. I wished I had listened to her.

However things were far from fine and to cover up my habit I found lodgings in a local cafe, the Ponderosa Cafe for £20 a week, food included and moved out from Granny's.

I was determined not to let her see what I was fast becoming. She was fine about the move since I was close by and I could pop in everyday at some stage to see her.

My room was sufficient for my needs but very soon it felt extraordinarily much like a comfortable prison cell, my cellmate's names despair and drinking.

During this time Mum and Bob and family moved from Thetford to Norwich and since it was a Saturday I helped with the move.

It was good to be together and I had a lot of fun that day, especially with my younger brother, Darren. He was, and still is, a good mannered and kind natured person.

There was, however, one incident that haunts me to this very day.

As I was helping him sort out his new bedroom I discovered a Bible and for some reason I was shocked.

"This yours Darren?" I held up the blue covered book. He suddenly looked very sheepish as though I discovered some hidden secret.

"Yes." He was clearly embarrassed as I began to laugh and mock him.

"You're not a bible basher are you?" I was roaring with laughter but I quickly realized that Darren had gone very quiet and I knew I'd hit a soft spot. Being the person I was, I was completely insensitive to his needs.

To this day I can still see the hurt in his eyes at what I had said and done. It was a shameful thing that I did that to him and to this day I firmly believe that I turned him away from his faith but at the time I just didn't care.

><>

The night job was easy once I had learnt to operate the various machinery used to chop and mince up the meats and spices used to make sausages and other products that churned out six days and nights a week.

Setting up the bowl chopping machines had to be done just right or else the very large, very sharp spinning blades that sliced and diced the meats would hit the metal sides of the bowl and shatter, sending razor like shards of metal everywhere.

Although there was safety devices in place it was still something you didn't want to be nearby to if this happened.

Once I was on shift and I had set up my machine I was basically left alone in what was called the Bowl Chopper Room. The room was adjacent to the factory floor but behind sets of heavy duty plastic curtains both to keep the noise levels from the main work force and also for safety.

As long as I kept pumping out the meat mixtures and then pushing the stainless steel trolleys with it in out to the receiving bay to be turned into sausages and other tasty foods, then I was left alone. Exactly how I liked it. I occasionally ventured out to get more products to work with but essentially I was alone.

My only companion on those long night shifts was usually a half bottle of Captain Morgan's rum, drank neat and straight from the bottle, which I kept tucked down the inside of my knee length work boots, a convenient place to secrete it. If anyone ever suspected that I was boozing on duty then I never heard of it.

My room at the café became a place of despair for me. I usually arrived back from work at about 6.30am and, unless I went out to see Granny then I wouldn't have hardly any contact with anyone else. Most nights before work I would take my meals in my room, either from the cafe below or a Chinese takeaway.

There was no one I could confide in, no friends to go and see and talk about my feelings. I was lonely on a planet of several billion people.

One Saturday I slipped up badly and went round Gran's whilst drunk. I can vividly remember how upset she was by this and how she tried to convince me to stop my drinking. After that I resolved to pack in the drink, once and for all, and stick with Gran's remedy, good old tap water!

For the next few weeks I tried as hard as I knew how to stop, short of seeking medical help. Granny checked me every day and now that the problem was out in the open I felt more in control of my life. I even began to hope a little once again.

But trouble was never far away from me and it soon rolled in from a totally unexpected direction.

CHAPTER TEN.

By working at the factory I made enough money to be able to buy an old yellow ford Cortina and I would simply drive about all over the place, listening to music and, of course, drinking as I drove. The car became a safe place for me and I spent more time in her than back at the cafe, glad to escape the confines of the four prison like walls. Many times I was blind drunk at the wheel and I once woke up in the car park behind the café with absolutely no idea of where I had been. It was that bad. But bad was becoming the normal for me.

One of the men I worked with on night shift, Terry, was a good kind of guy and actually lived on a Norfolk Broad's cruiser that was moored on the river Waveney at Beccles with his family. We got on quite well and one Saturday night he invited me to have a drink with him on board.

We had a great evening and towards the end he told me that he was selling the boat and getting a place on dry land. The kids needed schooling now and a boat was now no longer a good place for them to grow up on.

The idea of living on a boat suddenly appealed to me, anything to escape the room at the café. By the time I left that night we had agreed on a price of £3000, more than enough for a deposit on the house he wanted, and as far as I was concerned it was a done deal. We had shaken hands on the matter and that was enough for me.

I left that night full of excitement and hope as the thought of living on the boat had got hold of me. I could drink as much as I like and simply cruise along with no one to bother me at all. It seemed wonderful.

First thing Monday morning I went to my bank, applied for a loan of £3500and, since I met all the conditions, I walked out that very same day with the cash. The pile of ten and twenty pound notes made me feel the richest man alive! Never in my life had I had so much cash in my back pocket!

I decided there and then to go and see Terry and hand over the cash. Full of good will and already planning my first cruise along the Waveney River I parked my Cortina in the car park and crossed the marina to where the boat, my boat, was moored.

I caught sight of Terry on deck. I called over to him.

"I've got the cash, mate!" I was secretly betting that he would be as impressed as hell that I had got the cash so fast. I didnt want to hang around longer than I had to. The café now seemed more a prison cell than ever. I wanted the freedom of the river more than anything else and had already given a great deal of thought to my first party.

Terry stepped ashore to meet me. The look on his face soon dampened my spirit. He was a small, thin, ill looking man at the best of times, but at the moment he looked positively under the weather today. I had a sudden sinking feeling in the pit of my stomach, a premonition of sorts.

"Sorry, Gary, but I've changed my mind about things." He nodded

over his shoulder towards the boat, and lowered his voice to a whisper."
She's not happy about the deal." He meant his wife, a rather stern kind of
lady. It was obvious who ruled the roost in his house. Terry shrugged,
"Sorry mate but the deals off."

To be honest I used a few choice words to let him know what I
thought of him, his wife and the whole deal. All my plans were gone, sunk
without trace, no pun intended.

Terry retreated to the boat and I was left standing on the quayside
alone and fuming. As I walked back to my car I was very aware of the
weight of the £3500 cash in my pocket.

As I sat in my car I wondered what on earth I was going to do now. I
pulled the wad of cash of my jacket pocket and sat there, simply holding it.

Should I just take it back to the bank and give it back? I wasn't sure if
that was even possible and maybe I would have to pay some fee for taking
it back so fast.

Maybe I could look around the quay to see if there was another boat
up for sale? I couldn't remember seeing any signs up anywhere. Besides
where did you go to find out about buying a boat?

I pulled out my bottle of rum and sat there having a nice quite drink,
pondering what life had thrown at me. I hardly noticed the spirit going
down my neck.

A cold fury welled up in me as I sat there drinking and looking at
Terry's boat. I was absolutely seething with rage and contemplated giving
Terry a real hiding. How very unfair events had turned out yet again for me.
What on earth did I have to do to have a chance to have something good
happen to me? Was it really too much to ask, just for once?

I looked at the cash and decided there and then to keep £500, take the
week off work, and go on a drinking spree to blot out the whole episode.
The remaining £3000 I would take back next week.

The idea of spending any more time in the café really didn't do it for
me and so I asked Bob if I could borrow his four berth caravan for a while.
He agreed and all I needed was a place to park it up. I called one of the guys
who worked nights with me, Irish George who had once mentioned that he
had a large plot of land at the bottom of his garden and I could move in
there. During a late night tea break I'd had this idea about buying a camper
van and living in it having the freedom to move about whenever I wanted.

Irish George agreed, Bob brought the caravan over to Wangford,

Suffolk, and I was soon settled in at the bottom of the garden, the café history,

⨯⌒

The first week in the caravan was great. No one to bother me and there was a pub five minutes' walk away. I soon became a regular, lunch time and most evenings, and I drank to my heart's content, simply staggering back to the caravan and sleeping until I woke up.

When out drinking I would be like Doctor Jeckle and Hyde. One moment I would be the life and soul of the party. The next second I'd be depressed and lonely and feeling invisible in the crowd. Have you ever felt like a goldfish in a bowl staring out at life going by? That was me in a nutshell.

The week off work had turned into a second, then a third, but I hardly noticed this. My work wondered where I was and soon found that I had moved. They actually sent someone round to see me, as was their policy in such situations of unexplained absences. I was really somewhat rude to this person, who after all, was only trying to help.

A few days later I received written confirmation by a letter given to George at work, and hand delivered to me, that I had been formally dismissed from my job. I didnt give stuff by then. I had plenty of cash, a pub to drink in, and a place to live and sleep and eat.

⨯⌒

To explain my absence from working to my family I wove a story that I had won a few thousand pounds on the football pools and could afford to have a few weeks off work.

I lied to everyone, including Granny, something I regret even to this day. I was spiraling out of control but hardly noticed it anymore. I was like a leaf in a hurricanes grip.

As I drank I frittered away cash like water down a drain, pushing away all thoughts of what would happen when it was gone away from the present.

Very soon the caravan became a pit of despair, even worse than the room at the café I had been so desperate to escape. Something new was happening to me. For the first time in years I began to have dark, terrible thoughts of suicide.

The more I drank, the rage that was in me seemed to claw its way to the surface. A terrible boiling maelstrom of anger. Sometimes when I was drunk I would just stand there in the confines of the caravan and just scream with rage at the world in general, like a man possessed by legions of demons. People heard me some distance away and the local council received complaints from neighbors and contacted George to see what was happening.

Everything seemed so unfair. No Dad. No friends. No one to love me. In fact I seemed to have a dark habit of pushing away and hurting those who tried to get close. I was a loner by nature but desperately needed friends.

Much of the rage came back to the root of it all; having no Dad. I would often sit and weep for long hours at the hurt of it all. My life could've been so different if I'd had a Dad.

Often late at night, after a drinking spree, I would drive my Cortina as fast as I could through the back lanes, not caring if I crashed and died. I didn't quite have the courage to kill myself on purpose. My favorite trick was to drive fast and then turn off the headlights. Looking back now I can see Gods protective hand on my life. I should've been dead many times over.

One week I drove over to south Wales and to the Brecon Beacons area, sleeping in the car. I spent the days walking over the hills, searching for some kind of peace of mind. I wanted to avoid all human contact. I knew I was heading downhill fast and a part of me was in survival mode, frantically trying to come up with a solution to it all.

One very cold day I stood on the edge of an uneven cliff face and looked down the long, long drop to the jagged rocks at the bottom. I had been in utter despair all that night and it seemed as though there were voices calling for me to just die and end it all. Would there be peace then? I didn't know.

The wind was howling gale force, rain hitting my face like small pellets, stinging me, numbing my skin, as I stood there looking down. I inched forward, toes right on the edge, and slowly leaned into the wind like some free falling parachutist, arms outstretched. It suddenly seemed as though the wind was growing stronger, as if trying to push me back and away from the terrible danger of the long fall. Like God Himself was blowing me backwards.

To fall was certain death. I felt very calm and detached from it all.

I stood there for some time just leaning out into the wind, my life hanging by the sheerest of threads. A sudden numbing thought flashed across my mind; what happens if I don't die at the bottom and lay there severely injured and in pain?

Dying didn't worry me in that second but the thought of laying there for days suffering as I slowly died in a drawn out agonizing death suddenly petrified me badly.

I stepped back away from the entrance to the abyss and sat down on the rain soaked rocks, weeping at the nearness of it all. There had to be something better than this life I was leading.

I've no idea how long I sat there but by the time I made a move back to my car it was getting dark.

⋉⋊

As the money dwindled away my behavior became more erratic as each day passed and I rarely left the caravan now. I had stocked up on dozens of bottles of rum and snack food and simply drank and slept. Drank and slept.

Eventually I was down to the last few hundred pounds, nothing in the bank and was quickly running out of options as to what to do.

I had no job now, no friends at all. I'd upset the family as they had found out about my great tale about the cash. I couldn't face going to see Granny, as I knew she'd been badly upset by what I had done.

I have often wondered, looking back now at events, why I had never met any Christians or even anyone to help me. Where were all the good people hiding when I needed help? I always now encourage people to help those in need as there's millions of Gary's out there who just need a little tender loving care.

⋉⋊

I was reading a book, LEGIONAIRRE, by a man called Simon Murray and it was all about the legendary and infamous French Foreign Legion.

The Legion is run by France, staffed by French officers but is filled with men from almost every nation of earth. It's a top class, highly trained and motivated fighting force that's possibly the best in the world.

Most people have heard of Beau Gest running round in the desert with the camels battling the enemy. Laurel and Hardy even made a comedy where they joined La Legion.

As I read the book I was enthralled and captivated by the stories I found of the toughness and excitement, the camaraderie of the Legionnaires. It was place, so it seemed, where a man could lose himself and, almost, be born again into another life.

As I read, then re-read the book; I began to reason with myself. Why shouldn't I join? I had nothing to lose.

I had no hope, no future, no peace, and no friends. No one would miss me if I just upped and joined.

For several days I tossed and turned as I played the idea through my mind.

Nothing too loose if I went.

Nothing to gain if I stayed.

Finally I made up my mind after a long night drinking and talking to myself.

I decided to get to Paris, find a recruiting officer and join the French Foreign Legion!

Decision made, I slept soundly for the first time in weeks.

Since making my choice I was a man on a mission. I told no one of my plans and simply left the caravan in a right mess for Bob to sort out. I toyed with the idea of setting it on fire, giving it a Viking funeral as I had done with my old yellow VW beetle back in Germany. I decided against and just drove away to Thetford where my sister, Debby, lived and I left the car outside her flat then caught a National Express coach to London and from there an overnight coach to Paris.

The adventure had begun!

As the coach pulled into the big bus station situated on Avenue De General de Gaulle I never realized just how big Paris was. It was simply packed with people despite the lateness of the hour and cars, buses and late night revelers made me wonder if the city ever slept. I'd been to London many times late at night but there was something different about Paris. It was raining but that didn't seem to dampen the pace of life.

I had no plan except to find a recruitment office and sign on. The only problem was that I had no real idea where such an office was located. My first challenge.

I walked into an all-night café and ordered a beer and a toasted sandwich, ham and cheese, done as only the French can in one of those little machines behind the bar. The late crowd in there was a rough looking bunch and as I sat there, enjoying my toasty and beer, I felt right at home. There were prostitutes and some very obvious villains sitting in the shadows like something right out of an old black and white movie.

The barman, who looked as though he could handle just about

anything or anyone, spoke a little English and so I asked him for directions to the Legion recruiting office. He called over to an older man who looked tougher still, and introduced me. He spoke better English and had in fact served with the infamous 2ND REP, the Regiment Estranger de Parachutist, and the Foreign Legion Parachute regiment, based in Calvi on the island of Corsica. The very toughest of the tough.

We talked late into the night with lots of beer flowing, as I was regaled with incredible tales. If only a third of the stories were true I was still impressed. By early morning I was more positive than ever that this was for me. It was the Legion or nothing!

As dawn ebbed in I realized just how tired I was and found a small run down pension, a guesthouse of sorts, and booked in and was soon fast asleep, dreaming of heroic adventures.

The next morning I set off to find the address I had been given for the main recruitment office in Paris, Fort de Nogent.

My French was practically non-existent so I simply produced the hand written address to a passerby, Fort de Nogent, Poste d'information et de recruitement de la Légion estrangère. 94120 Fontenay sous-bois.

I got very surprised looks from more than a few folks as I walked across Paris, asking directions as I went. It took me the best part of the day to hike through the sprawling suburbs of the great city. I was in no great hurry and stopped once or twice for beers and some more of those wonderful toasted sandwiches.

Finally, around 3pm, I found what I had been looking for, Fort de Nogent, looking strangely out of place in the middle of a built up area. Tall concrete walls loomed above me and I stopped in front of the twin wooden gates. A small plaque told me I had found the right place.

I moved away a few meters and sat down on a small low wall. This was it. I sat there for a few minutes just staring at the twin doors, butterflies doing loop the loop in my stomach as nerves got hold of me.

I stood and began to walk to the gates, a surge of fear flashing through me as I knocked on the gates and waited for whatever was going to happen next.

Almost immediately the gates opened and I had my first sight of a Foreign Legionnaire as he looked me up and down, gave me a cold hard look, then stepped aside and beckoned me in.

Taking a pearl divers deep breath I stepped into the unknown.

There is a time-honored routine for all those who dare to join the Legion.

You are taken in and asked in your own language why you are here, just to make sure you are in the right place and haven't just wandered in by mistake.

Once that's sorted then all of your worldly goods are taken from you. Your passport, money, clothing and luggage, everything of a personal nature, all gone within the first hour or so of arrival.

I was ordered to strip off my civilian clothing and was handed a pile of green army fatigues, similar to US army greens. I was surprised to find that they smelt clean. I was then given washing gear, all the usual stuff needed by a guy. No more, no less.

I was told that all food and clothing would be supplied for me now that the Legion was my home.

The first few days were spent in a whirlwind of activity as I settled into life in the Fort. Everything was both familiar and unfamiliar at one and the same time.

We were put to work in the large mess hall serving and cleaning pots and tables. I was told that no civilians did this job that the Legion looked after itself. As we washed and cleaned up it gave me a good chance to observe the rest of the men there as we hustled to get the work done under the watchful eyes of the NCO's in charge of us.

On my second night there I watched with envy as a large group of maybe 150 men was gathered in the huge courtyard and addressed by the camp commandant. These men were off tonight for the journey by train down to Aubagne, southern France, and a few kilometers from Marseilles, where the selection process began in earnest. They looked a ragged bunch to say the very least. It seemed that every week or so, when there was enough gathered, then another group was dispatched south for selection.

As I watched them board busses form the journey to the train station I could only guess how long it would be before I, too, made the journey.

But until then we would be worked hard, Legion style.

In the large open plan barracks we lived in you could hear a multitude of languages spoken. English, Spanish, German, Arabic, African,

Yugoslavian, and Russian were just a few.

Two lads I got to know had walked and hitch hiked hundreds of miles all the way from the then Yugoslavia. I gathered they had been in some trouble there and had done a runner. I didn't ask the reasons why they had bugged out.

An older guy, an American called Frank, shared the bunk above mine and was quite chatty. He was an ex- US marine and just couldn't settle down. He was at least 40 but was very fit indeed and not one to mess with.

Many of my fellow recruits had hard looking faces. Some were ex-soldiers who couldn't settle down. Others were just nasty bits of work, full stop. Among these men I felt like a small puppy. I had been in a few fights in my time but what I saw here made me cringe. I hoped my worries didn't show or else I would be a target. They would smell fear like a shark sensing blood. There was no room for weakness in the Legion.

There was a great deal of swaggering and posturing, as some men were out to prove how tough they were. Each night there were some very nasty fights as tempers flared and offence taken. Thefts were regularly taking place in the barracks, hardly surprising given the mix of men. Mainly small items were lifted, easily concealed and quickly sold for cash, and some of the fights were over this as accusations were made and denied.

There was one young lad who had run away to join the Legion. His girlfriend had left him and, heartbroken, he had come to forget his past. How classic is that? Just like something out of a novel but very true. I've often wondered what happened to him.

As the days passed we began to hear rumors that another batch of recruits were going to be sent off in the next few days on the long overnight train down to Marseilles then onto Aubagne to begin selection proper. The news crackled throughout the Fort as the word spread. Excitement was crackling like electricity before a good old-fashioned thunderstorm.

It suddenly felt great to be alive and kicking. I looked around at all the guys and I felt a wave of pride to be a part of it all. It was good to simply be there.

I remember one day we had been over at the officer's mess, cleaning and polishing glasses, under the watchful eyes of a corporal. There was about twenty of us there with a lot of lighthearted banter going on. When we had finished the corporal decided to give us a lesson in how to march. We formed up in two ranks and he explained what he wanted us to do. Very simple and easy to understand. I knew all about marching having been drilled by a Grenadier Guards trained Drill sergeant back in the RMP. Straightforward.

On the command 'Marche' I moved off at 120 paces a minutes British Army style, arms shoulder high, chin up, gut in, and as I had been trained.

The corporal and everyone else in the group were amazed as I sped away like a greyhound on heat. The corporal yelled for me to stop and come back! What I never realized is that the Legion marches at 88 paces per minute, a slower more dignified way. I felt extremely silly but everyone had a good-natured laugh at me.

At teatime we were informed that we would be leaving the very next evening. A huge cheer went up from the long rows of tables where we sat, a buzz of excitement. Talk that night was of the future.

I remember that evening I went to the television room to escape the confines of the barracks. There was a music video showing by a band named Toto. It was a song that I will never forget and was called Africa and somehow summed up the journey I was now on. Tomorrow night at this very time I would be on a train heading for adventure.

I had trouble sleeping that night.

Straight after breakfast the whole detachment was marched across to the main administration block for a very important event; the signing of the 5-year Legion contract.

This is a simple two-page document. The first page contains personal data with the terms and conditions of service explained on page two. A translation of page two follows the contract so the potential Legionnaire is in no doubt as to what he is signing up for.

I marched into the adjutant's office very smartly, signed the contract without even asking a single question, about turned and left. As far as I was concerned that was it. I was in!

Finally the hour arrived to leave. We had a last meal in the large canteen. I wouldn't be sad to see the back of that particular place. Hours had been spent cleaning up tables and scrubbing pot and pans. During the last two weeks there had been a steady stream of new men coming in who in turn would have to wait their turn before making the journey. I could see the same open-eyed stares as they watched events unfold, as we made ready to leave. I was keyed up, tingling with excitement, buzzing like a bee.

We had each been issued with old army greatcoats and given green berets to wear to try and make us look a bit smarter.

Several coaches arrived and we were loaded on board for the journey to the Gare De Lyon train station.

Once there we were pushed into a vague resemblance of order by the NCO's with us and with a curt command, were marched inside the train station. I can still vividly see the thousands of passengers staring at us with unashamed curiosity as we entered the station, marching in formation, then headed for the departure platform. We all had shaved heads by now and must have looked a real sight. Already I was feeling like the tip of the sword.

The journey would last most of the night, hopefully arriving at the southern seaport city of Marseilles early next morning. Many of us anticipating a thirsty night's travel had purchased huge amounts of beer and spirit and foodstuffs. Soon the air in the carriages was blue with the acrid smoke from hundreds of gitanes cigarettes, since these were given freely as part of pay and rations.

Soon we were all settled in, drinking and eating and telling huge tales of past exploits. Sitting there in the carriage watching these companions of mine I had to fight back the urge to cry as I had this huge sense of belonging to a family; The French Foreign Legion.

And here I was, heading off to begin a five-year contract with the most infamous group of men on the earth. Life couldn't have been better at that moment in time. No one that I knew had any idea where Gary Wayne Ernest Moore was at that precise time. I had even signed my contact under another name something offered to every man who joins.

And that suited me down to the ground.

We arrived very early more than worse for wear after a hard nights drinking. The smell of vomit clung to us like a cheap aftershave, evidence of the journeys excesses. A night spent on a train like that is not to be made a habit of!

We were met at the station by more buses and ferried away to Aubagne, the Legions official headquarters.

The camp at Aubagne was big and looked just like any other military camp the world over. Strange yet familiar.

Tall, spik and span living quarters, groups of men hurrying about being shouted at by NCO's. A whole lot of action going on with purpose and vigour as military life ebbed and flowed with a mood and menace of its own.

We stood there for a few short seconds, gathering kit; then all hell broke loose as the NCO's herded us towards the living blocks. We didn't walk, we ran, even up the stairs, even to our rooms and arrived gasping and sweating.

The rooms were large but the bunk beds were four high, the top bunk at least sixteen feet above ground.

Many of the occupants had been there a while going through the selection process and so had settled in, taking the lower, and safer, bunks. It was sardine time and tempers soon flared and a full on fight developed within minutes.

It was short, sharp and very nasty. All over a sleeping space.

The whole function of Aubagne was to weed out the weakest links before proper training began and to this purpose there was a whole series of tests designed to winkle out those unsuitable to wear the coveted Kepi Blanc.

There was a battery of aptitude tests, medical examinations and long sessions being questioned by the Legion internal security service, known as the Gestapo, to screen out any potential trouble. There were also the Interpol police checks. Gone were the days when murderers could vanish into the Legions ranks with ease.

Many of us thought that just by signing the contract back in Paris that we were in for good not knowing it was provisional subject to training. Many were in for a shock as the group was whittled down on an almost daily basis.

During times of conflict the Legion would fling open its very broad gates and welcome all, the same as any army. But during relative peacetime the standards are raised and strictly adhered too. Quality not quantity becomes the order of the day.

Many of the tests puzzled me, I must admit and I know that many of the others lads had the same problems.

As you progress towards passing you change from a yellow armband, to green and then finally to red.

For those who failed it was always the same. One second they would be with you, next called away and vanished like they never existed except in memory. Missing faces at mealtimes became a depressing feature. For some it was a relief to be discharged as the reality of Legion life sunk home. Many would've clearly never survived basic training.

For others it was the worst possible outcome as hopes and aspirations died a sudden and violent death. Many had nowhere else to go to and I have wondered many times what happened to them.

As the weeks passed I moved up to yellow, then green, by now confidant that I was doing well. I should have known better.

One morning as we were cleaning the mess hall just after breakfast had finished, there was a whisper of rumor that there was a batch of three more to be released from contract because of failure in the latest tests. No one knew who they were but the whispers were sometimes fairly accurate. And today it was predicted that there was to be an Englishman.

All of us were fairly fit in body but it was also the mind that was just as important to the Legion. Mental toughness can overcome the physical side of things. If your mind were focused then your body would follow no matter what you were called on to do.

Just after lunch three names were called out, one of them mine and I thought it was just another work detail, but as we were taken towards the administration block I suddenly felt like a sick dog heading to the vets where a needle waited for me. I just knew that I was about to be binned. I could see the same thoughts on the faces of the other guys. Bad news time.

After a brief wait I was ushered into a small office. An officer sat there, typically French, the ever-present Gitanes cigarette smoking away, and very serious looking. I could hardly breathe I was so panicky and filled with dread at what I knew was coming my way.

I stood at attention before him, best RMP style.

He cleared his throat and spoke in very good English.

"You are no good to us. Your contract has been terminated." He paused and, with a flourish, scribbled something on the papers spread before him on his desk. He didn't even look at me." You are free to leave the Legion."

"You can't do this!" I almost shouted. "I want to be a Legionnaire. Nothing else!"

The officer gave me a long cold stare." You're out-now go!" he nodded to the door as though I was something unpleasant. The senior NCO with us tensed, ready for trouble.

I seriously thought about arguing the point but the look on his face said if all, his words ringing in my ears,' you're no good to us'.

I about turned and marched out, my own way of telling him where he could stuff things.

Within the hour I was taken in a ridiculously large bus for just the three of us being kicked out, to the local train station for the overnight back to Paris. I was left on the platform clutching my one way ticket, my suitcase, some cash from the pay I had received, and that was that. The two lads with me were from Belgium and looked as desolate as I felt. It was a bad time standing there.

On the train as we travelled through the night, it was decided that if the Legion wouldn't have us, then we'd find someone who would. So it was determined over beer and Gitanes that on arrival in Paris we'd go to one of the many mercenary recruiters and see what we could get into. Afghanistan was in full swing with the Russian invasion taking place and there was always something going on in Africa. There had to be something to get involved with. There was a terrible, gnawing desperation flowing through my veins that night on the train as though hope was being strangled.

As the overnight express rumbled through the long, dark night I remember staring out at the darkened countryside, the occasional lights flashing past in some small hamlet. The window was mirror-like and all I could see was my reflection looking right back at me.

What did I see?

A failure. A waste of space. How had life gone so wrong, I asked myself yet again?

I had failed in my attempt to join the Legion. I still couldn't quite take it in. but this was real life, real time.

I mused on all that had taken place in my life. All the good intentions, trying hard yet, always without fail, falling short of what was needed. It was as though some divine hand was against me all the time.

Failed in family, in love, in Army, in the Legion.

As I stared at my face in the mirror the all too familiar bitterness at never knowing my Dad welled up, yet again, tears stinging my eyes. I was very glad that the two others were drunk and fast asleep. I stepped out into the empty corridor, stood by the doors, and wept and wept, pain oozing out of every pour in my body. I was wounded and hurting and didn't know how to be healed.

I was all alone, once again, travelling through the darkness of a lonely life.

$$\rightarrowtail\!\!\bigcirc$$

CHAPTER ELEVEN

My first visit to Paris, just a few weeks earlier, had been to join the French foreign Legion and I had been full of hope for the future, moving away from the past I was running hard from. Heady times as the pathway ahead seemed exciting and full of challenge, as if for once I was master of my destiny and not a wave, tossed about by every gust of wind.

As the train pulled into Paris, a cold, hard rain was driving down in a way that would've impressed Noah. The morning was dark and very unwelcoming as if the City knew that we had failed and didnt want us back, frowning in disapproval. I still vividly remembered the night we had left for Aubagne, full of hope and proud to be a part of the Legion. Now I almost felt ashamed as if fellow passengers around me knew of my failure.

One of the guys had an address of a bar known to be a contact point for soldiers of fortune seeking out employment for their skills in their rather unique trade. You couldn't just walk into the job center and ask for a job killing people. That could get you into trouble. Certain discretion was needed.

We hopped onto the Metro, crossing Paris underground, surfacing some time later like untidy damp moles under the grey rain filled sky not far from our destination.

The bar was open for business even at such an early hour, supposedly to serve coffee but we managed to get a round of beers in to start the day properly. We found a table at the back of the bar and sat down. It was a bit of a dump but it was dry and warm. The ashtray on the table was full and overflowing.

My two companions, Jean-Paul and Andre, were both chains smokers and soon filled our corner of the room with the blue acrid smoke that is a trademark of Gitanes. My eyes soon stung and very watering badly. I smoked occasionally but couldn't handle these tough French cigarettes.

It was decided that Jean-Paul, or JP for short, would make the move to ask the barman about the modus operandi for getting introduced to the mercenary recruiters. As none of us had ever done such a thing before we were unsure as to how you actually did it. It wasn't an everyday occurrence.

In Hollywood films there is always one rough looking character, wearing shades with the obligatory scar on his tanned face, to ask in such situations. Someone very obvious to whom the hero go straight too and asks, get an answer and then get on with the job of saving the world in ninety minutes.

But here in this bar they all looked rough and even the few ladies there had scars on their faces! Not the place to take your mother for Sunday lunch.

JP moved across to the bar and spoke quietly to the barman for several minutes. When he came back, he looked very glum.

"Right place, wrong time." He began. "The guy we need won't be here for a few days, if he comes at all. However," he held a small scrap of paper up like a winning lottery ticket," I do have another address. "

This time it was a ninth floor flat in the middle of a rundown housing estate. I'd never seen such a mess in my life. It didn't look like the Paris the tourists see. Drab and depressive I was struck by the large number of Arabs on the streets and dogs that ran wild. I shuddered to think what this was like at night.

Again no luck but we were given yet another address to try a number of miles outside of Paris, this time for a small fee. Apparently the authorities had been cracking down on the mercenary trade and so those we needed to see were elusive.

By now it was early evening so we pooled our cash together and took a triple room in a seedy hotel that appeared exactly how I was starting to feel and appear; run down and futureless and very shabby.

After a few beers we turned in for the night hoping that tomorrow would bring better luck than today. I was running out of options and hope was also in short supply.

><>

The train journey the next day took 2-3 hours, longer than I expected and I wasn't quite sure where we were going until the stations sign for TOURS rolled into view. I'd had this sinking feeling since getting up that all was not going to go to plan as though events were moving without me having any say in what took place. I called it the Pinocchio syndrome.

JP and Andre had been talking all the way down in their native language and I had no idea what they were on about. I had this suspicion that some of it was about yours truly, as if they were planning something. I was uncomfortable and wary and I had the feeling I knew why.

At the hotel last night I had made the mistake of letting them see how much cash I had, which wasn't a lot, but more than they had. Something had changed last night and I didn't like it. I had slept very lightly just in case, my knife to hand.

JP I liked and got on well with but there was something sinister about Andre and I knew full well that JP was frightened of him for some reason, even though he was bigger and fitter.

As we walked from the station into the town looking for the address I made sure that I kept my knife handy and quickly accessible. I had a nose for trouble and something stank.

Once again we found ourselves in a bar, sipping nice beer, covered in smoke. JP approached the barman as usual and from where we sat it looked as if things were going well. The pair were smiling and nodding.

JP returned, all smiles. He nodded across to the barman who was speaking into a telephone hidden behind the bar counter.

"He's calling the guy we need to see."

A flash of excitement hit us all and a sudden surge of hope washed through me, like a strong breath of dying embers.

I wondered where we might be able to go. Afghanistan or Africa was the two top destinations for mercenaries at the time as well as a number of lesser-known conflicts around the globe.

As I sipped my beer, making it last, I decided that I would go anywhere and anyplace I could.

Beggars can't be choosy.

How true that was to turn out to be.

We didn't have too long to wait to see the results of the barman's 'phone call and barely fifteen minutes later a small, smartly dressed man walked in, looked at the barman who, in turn, nodded to where we sat. He walked over with the confidence of one who can take care of himself and sat down at table with us. No introductions were made. He just started to talk and that was that.

He was a grim faced sort of man with the typical aloofness of the French. He spoke rapidly and I had no idea what he was saying at all. Even the boys had trouble keeping up with him.

"You speak English?" I asked hopefully. He nodded, paused, and then spoke just as fast.

"I am sorry you have had a wasted trip here," he shrugged and didn't sound as if he meant it." If you had been here two days ago I would've had work for you all." He lit a Gitanes, a national French sporting pastime.

" Now there is nothing. Perhaps a in a few weeks' time?" he shrugged in a very Gaelic way, stood and began to leave us. I guess it was good of him to even come to see us.

As he moved away I called after him." Where was the work going too?" I just had to know or else it would haunt me forever.

"Afghanistan." He called over his shoulder, and then was gone.

Disappointment hung over us like a thick damp cloud as we sat there barely able to take it in. Words didn't seem to have any meaning in those few minutes of silence. I finished my beer and felt as empty as the glass.

We'd run out of options now, as we had no more names or places to check out. To miss out on the work out to Afghanistan by just a few hours was bad luck to say the very least and was as simple as that.

Looking back at the conflict raging in that unhappy land I am rather glad that I never did get there. It was a vicious war with no mercy given by either side or some of the worst atrocities ever recorded by mankind took place there, by both sides.

I decided there and then to split up with the lads, as there really was no future with them. We had found ourselves in a unique situation after being kicked out of the Legion and would never have met otherwise.

I brought the subject up." What are you two guys going to do now?" the hint very clear that we were parting company.

It was JP who answered for both of them. "Head back home, maybe Paris, look for work…"he trailed off his words and shrugged. They had as much idea as I had. None.

All of us had run away from troubles in our pasts, the reasons various and no doubt complicated and the last thing we wanted was to have to go back to our former lives. I didn't know what the guy's stories were but I could imagine they weren't too dissimilar from my own.

I had nothing or no one to go back to in the UK. All my bridges had been not so much burnt down as blown up and I could expect no help from anyone.

I knew that when I split from the lads that I would be totally alone on this planet, but somehow, in that moment, I didn't give a damn.

><>

We said our farewells outside the train station under a sky, which had lightened considerably since yesterday. It was rain free and for that I was glad. The guys were heading back to Paris and from there? Who knew what would happen next.

I had a return ticket, which we changed at the office, with JP's help, for an open return, as I had said that I was going to hang around for a few days. It was a bit of a lie, as I had no idea what I was going to do. But one thing was for certain and that was that I badly needed a drink and to get blindingly drunk. It was no solution to anything whatsoever but at least I would forget about things for a few hours.

So I went on a drinking spree blowing the last of my cash, leaving me broke in a foreign country. I had long since decided that if I ever got short of cash then I would simply mug someone. Easy money. I'd done it before and knew I could do it again if need be.

At some stage I also lost my train ticket back to Paris and so I was both broke and stranded. When I finally sobered up I found, much to my surprise, that I was also many miles away from where I started, the how of it all I had no idea. It was also three days later!

The next few nights and days were a blur as I slept rough feeling terrible. I ate some sticks of bread that I had tucked away in my small suitcase before the drinking started. I was glad that I did, as that was all that I had to eat, and even this was hard and stale.

I decided to hitch hike and see where I ended up, not quite sure where I was to begin with. I had no map and no idea.

I was in an awful state, unwashed and rough looking and I could smell myself, and had that sticky, greasy feeling. I was that bad.

So I stood by the side of the road and stuck out my thumb in the time honored tradition and waited for a lift, even managing to smile most of the time.

Several hours I was still standing there and no wonder with the state I was in. Several cars slowed but took one look at me and sped off, followed by a stream of dreadful cursing from me, at the top of my voice.

Finally after several hours a car did stop and pull over in the lay-by next to me; it was the police!

What was the law on hitching in France I wondered as they climbed out and began to question me very firmly? In fact they were really quite rude to me.

I pleaded ignorance and then they realized I was a foreigner and then tried English which worked well. So I explained events of the last weeks and days, of the Legion and so on, up until this very point in time. I also tried to bluff it out with them and said that I was on the way to Paris to meet some friends. I could see they didn't believe a word I said.

Unfortunately for me I was actually heading completely the wrong way to Paris, which was north, and I was going south, on the main A10 road that led down to Bordeaux.

The senior cop was a polite kind of guy, and he suggested that I head to Bordeaux, which was far closer than Paris, and go to the British Consulate there and ask for help in getting back to England.

I smiled a lot and thanked him for his kind help but had no intention of going home even if I could've done.

The cops drove off leaving me by the roadside and I swore after them as well, but considerably quieter than normal!

I realized that no one was going to stop with me looking like the living dead and it was also starting to get dusky, daylight draining away. I needed a place to sleep that night and had to find somewhere safe. So I began to walk.

It seemed that with every step I took that a little more hope drained out of my feet and very soon I was in the deepest pit of despair I had ever known in my life. It felt as though my very soul was being sucked out of me, like life spilling from an open gunshot wound.

I couldn't see any future for me as I plodded along the roadside, cars speeding past me dangerously close on occasion. I was tired, hungry, dirty, and smelly and didn't care if I lived or died. I was in a quicksand of despair with no one to pull me out.

I began to see colorful, vivid pictures of my family; Mum and Bob. Debbie and Darren and little baby Rachel and of course my beloved Granny Moore. I realized with a shock that I had never told any of them, except Granny, that I loved them or even cared for them! Never, not once. I just couldn't.

WHY?

Hurt welled up in me, writhing like a coiled snake and I just broke down on the roadside verge, sobbing in absolute and total anguish as I realized what a complete and total mess up I had made of my life.

Deep down all I wanted was to love and be loved but somewhere along the road of my life I'd become hardened and cold and very uncaring in my dealing with people. It was if a heart of stone had transplanted into what should've been there.

I had hated turning into the man that I was that day but didn't have a clue how to stop or change the transformation from happy little boy playing with my Granddad in the back garden in Beccles, into the terrible man that I was today, full of rage and anger and violence of thought and act.

What had gone so wrong?

✠

It was pitch black by the time I'd found a place to doss down for the night. A low wall a few meters away from the road offered me shelter from passing cars and, more importantly, anyone on foot who might come across me. At night I treated everyone as potentially hostile and took no chances. Attack first and apologize later, if at all.

It was a nice night with every star clear and seemingly very close and I promised myself that one day I would learn all their names. The moon was full and showered enough light to enable me to make a small camp, as if trying to help me out in some small way. I glanced around the heavens, my own personal planetarium spread majestically above me. Not a cloud in the sky. Good, as that meant no rain.

As I lay there on my sleeping bag I just couldn't get the policeman's words out of my head about the consulate at Bordeaux and me trying to get home. Even if I managed to get home and faced the music about the money and all my lies, would anyone want me back? I had hurt and offended so many.

I doubted even Granny would have me back when I had lied constantly and consistently to her. A lie is a robbery with words.

I turned over trying to get warm, suddenly experiencing the sensation that the temperature had dropped several degrees very fast as though I had just walked into a fridge.

Then I felt, rather than sensed it; I wasn't alone here in the dark. I sat up, and was off the bag in an instant and on my feet, knife in hand. I was acutely aware that there were unseen eyes watching me from the darkness; dangerous, malevolent sinister forces that wanted to destroy and kill me and was moving closer by the moment, preparing to attack.

I experienced such a terror in those minutes that I was almost sobbing in fear, and grabbing my gear, I jumped the wall, ran out and into the light of the street lamps, moving quickly from darkness to solid light.

I was like a small child frightened awake by a sudden unexplained noise in the night, trying to get under blankets for safety.

It felt as though evil had taken on solid form and substance and was intent of hurting me, maybe taking my life, and was out there just behind the wall, as if unable to step out into light for fear of being exposed.

It was 2.30am as I stood there by the roadside, alone and very afraid and I decided there and then that I wanted to get back to Norwich and face any consequence that I had to, and make any apology that had to be made to right the wrongs. I couldn't stop sobbing such was the terror that had gripped me like a small finger in a vice, glancing around in all directions in case they, it, came from behind.

It was as though the sudden terror had brought me back to my senses, the shock of it all bringing reality into sharp, vivid focus.

But how to get home? How to make amends for all I'd done?

Like a major dam bursting I began to weep and weep, feeling as lost and helpless as a newborn baby left on the side of a dangerous road. I just didn't know how to handle things anymore, so I did something that I'd never done knowingly before in my life; I prayed!

I stood there, looked to the heavens and said out loud; "Oh God, get me home!" then added a softer "Please."

By home I was thinking of Norwich, England but God heard my heart instead and decided to perform a little miracle, in the early hours of a French morning.

A peace touched my heart as I finished saying those few short words and I distinctly remember wiping my eyes, suddenly knowing deep down that everything had just been taken care of. How, I had no idea. Just a deep-seated knowing that it had. I blew my nose on my sleeve and sighed, the fear gone, as if someone bigger than me was with me, more than able to protect me from anything in the world.

As I stood there on the roadside it was totally deserted with no sign of life anywhere, even though I was on the outskirts of a small town I had tramped through hours before.

No cars had passed me in the time I had been standing here, not surprising considering the time of day. I began to walk, mainly to keep warm as a chill had started to creep into me and I was nearly shivering. I had no idea how to get to Bordeaux and the British Consulate there and was thinking about this when the car pulled up right next to me, startling me completely as I'd never even heard the car's engine.

It was simply there as if it had been transported down from the star ship USS Enterprise.

The driver's window rolled down and an older man, white haired with a large, bushy moustache, spoke to me in English, with no trace of a French accent!

"I am going to Bordeaux. Can I offer you a lift?"

For several seconds I stood there, speech gone as if robbed, in absolute surprise at the offer. Was it a coincidence that I had just prayed a rather desperate prayer a few minutes earlier and now a car had stopped, going exactly where I needed to get too?

"Yes, I do." I managed to get out. I opened the back door and placed my small suitcase on the back seat, then climbed into the front seat next to the driver, and off we went.

Looking back I believe it was an Angel sent to help in a time of need.

I nodded to the driver," Thanks for stopping." I tried to make polite small talk but the driver simply shrugged and said, "OK," as if he'd run out of words to say.

The cars heater was on full blast against the chill and I soon found that my eyes were getting heavier and heavier as sleep ebbed in like a rising tide, and just as unstoppable. I soon drifted off to a comfortable sleep, wonderfully warm and safe, even in the car with a complete stranger.

A kind of peace I had never known before.

For how long I had been asleep or how far we had travelled, I had no idea. I awoke feeling so incredibly refreshed and rested it was as though I had slept in the finest bed for days on end and had never been through the trials of late.

The car was slowing down, moving off the main road, and then turning down a smaller road. Houses and shops lined the road on each side, a few solitary bedrooms lights on in houses.

It was still dark but now we were in a large town the streets empty except for parked cars and a few early morning workers heading off for their days toil. All the shops were dark and empty; except for a bakery we passed which threw delicious smells of fresh baked bread at us as we drove by. The aroma tasted good.

"Is this Bordeaux?" I asked. The driver nodded his reply and smiled. We turned one more corner, and then pulled to a stop, handbrake rasping on loudly.

"Ok, "said the driver," I can take you no further. It's up to you now." He smiled and held out his hand and I found that he had one of the most powerful grips in my life. His handshake way outperformed his apparent age.

I retrieved my suitcase then leaned back inside the car. "Thankyou." was all I said.

The driver nodded then drove off, the engine really quite loud in the early morning silence, sounding like some ancient diesel tractor, and I wondered how on earth I hadn't heard him coming earlier? Strange.

Dawn was just flushing the sky a rather nice pink and there was the smell of freshly baked bread on the still morning air, reminding me just how hungry I was.

I stood there for a while not sure what to do next. There was a wooden bench behind me so I sat down, my mind struggling to make a plan of action.

The light of day was getting brighter by the minute, allowing me to see my surrounding clearly.

A tall stone building was directly in front of me, a row of what looked like brass nameplates to one side of the entrance, dull in the low light and dew. I had good eyesight but I couldn't make out the wording as yet.

After the warmth of the car and the lovely sleep I had enjoyed I was beginning to feel the pre-dawn chill, so I began to walk around the immediate area of the bench, trying to generate some heat. I looked in shop windows as I strolled, keeping an eye on the bench and my case.

On my second circuit of the bench it was light enough to see clearly and as I came by the brass nameplate I paused to check the names-

-And very nearly fell over in complete shock.

I had been dropped right outside the British Consulate!

✗◯

CHAPTER TWELVE.

I spent the next few hours before the official opening time of the British Consulate-Generals offices, a dignified and sensible 09.30am, wandering through the streets of Bordeaux, to a certain extent in a slight state of shock at how events were unfolding before me.

What on earth were the chances of being dropped right outside the very building I so desperately needed to find, by a complete stranger who could not possibly have any kind of prior knowledge about anything to do with my life and immediate circumstances? How many billions to one odds did that come too? Was it simply an amazing stroke of luck, or was it something else?

I knew for a cast iron solid fact that I hadn't said a single thing to the driver about my life, or where I even wanted to go. It was becoming more mysterious by the second and I just couldn't shake it out of my head. It was as though there was a plan unfolding outside of my understanding and I wasn't in on it, just a vague awareness like a half remembered dream.

Come to that, I found it eerie and a little scary when I thought about the car itself. It had just, well, appeared right next to me, no noise or anything. Just there and it just happened to be going to Bordeaux and just happened to stop outside the Consulate.

I had a distinct feeling that someone was sorting things out for me.

117

But who, that was the question. Could it have of been the prayer I muttered under the heavens? The possibility seemed to have substance to it. Maybe God had heard me after all? I had no idea.

As I walked along those wide-open boulevards of Bordeaux, terrible pangs of loneliness gripped me quite hard as I watched normal people going about their everyday business and daily lives. For once, normal seemed good to me.

Men in smart suits walking briskly to work in offices and shops. Ladies off to get the groceries in, consulting lists as they walked on autopilot, or maybe to buy a new dress. Young children dressed in uniforms heading off to school without a real care in the world, laughing and chattering as only the young can do. I felt like a visitor from a far off world, separate from the rest of humanity moving around me, cloaked by a force field and invisible to the naked eye.

I sat on a nice wooden bench near a park. A bus stop was a few meters away, citizens waiting patiently for the next arrival. I people watched, a habit I have to this day, as life ebbed and flowed around me, all in glorious colour and surround sound.

A Mother and Father with a small toddler ambled slowly by on the way to the park. Laughter spilled from the little boy as he stepped along, hand held in a tight grasp inside his Fathers hand. His steps were small and unsure but each one a victory for him, both pleasing and frightening at the same time and the look on his small round face was a pleasure to see.

I smiled at the sight and the Father caught my eye and grinned proudly back. He said something to me and I just smiled and nodded back, no idea what he had just said, but it seemed to do the trick. Somehow I had been adopted momentarily into their small tight family by the shared instant of joy.

As they moved past and into the park tears filled my eyes uninvited and I thought, for a second, that I was going to die right there and then as my grief at being dad-less struck me very hard, like a blow from a robber in the dark to the back of the head. I was thankful that I had been sitting at the time.

I heard the boy's laughter one last time and it very nearly pushed me over the edge of reason.

How could anyone leave a child alone in the world? It was the height of cruelty to condemn a child to a life sentence of pain and inconsolable rejection for which there was no known cure. It was like injecting someone with the plague and then walking off, taking the only antidote known to man with them.

I checked the time and hurried off to the Consulate, not having a clue what was going to happen next.

When I eventually got to see someone face to face inside the offices of the British Consulate-General after a bit of a wait, I was in for a very rude surprise, like coming home to find that the locks had all been changed on your house.

I had, like many others who find themselves in dire straits abroad, been under the false illusion that the Embassies and consulates are there solely to get folks out of trouble, mainly of their own design and making, and will therefore move heaven and earth to cater for our every whim, because we're fellow Brits abroad.

WRONG!

The lady I saw was as helpful as it was possible to be and polite to the point of being painful, yet very firm; there was only so much they could do to help me. I soon found out that it wasn't very much at all.

I explained in detail my situation, leaving nothing out, a confession of sorts, from the drinking to the legion to the mercenary job hunt. I tried my hardest to get her to understand that I needed to get home, to sort things out as my greatest desire on this earth. I wonder now how many times she had heard the same story, but dressed in a different skin.

The lady listened, nodding in all the right places, even sighing here and there, which gave me hope that she had a caring heart and would help, quickly.

Was there someone who could send me some cash to help me make the journey home? She asked politely, as the consulate couldn't just pay passage for everyone who came through its doors. Was there anyone?

I was unusually honest with her in my replies, part of my new turning away from the past.

I didn't know my mum's new address or the new telephone number. Of course I could describe the place, but a number or name or name of the street? Sorry, couldn't help. The truth.

My Granny didn't have a telephone. The truth.

There were no friends to call. The truth.

"Surely there has to be someone to ask?" she sounded politely incredulous with my account of things.

"There is no one. That's the mess I've made of my life." I don't think I had ever been so honest and frank in all my life. I felt like a prisoner about to be sentenced making one last desperate plea for clemency to a hard faced jury.

I had been in the interview room for twenty-five minutes before sentence was passed on me.

"I am terribly sorry, Mr. Moore, we can only help in exceptional circumstances." She smiled as if that would soften the blow. "Sorry about that."

"So what's 'exceptional circumstances' then?" I pleaded from the heart." I have no money for food, nowhere to stay and no chance of getting either. What do I have to do to get help?" I tried to keep my voice calm, as I knew that if I got angry then I would stand no chance ever of help.

The poor lady caught the mood of my desperation and promised to have a 'word' with someone and I should come back later that day. They were, she informed me, open until 5.30pm.

I thanked her and left to tramp the streets of Bordeaux, despair as close on my heels as a snapping dog.

Outside on the streets it was lunchtime and, the French being so very French, enjoyed their food to the fullest.

Everywhere I looked there seemed to be eateries, restaurants and always street vendors selling all kinds of goodies; people munching on long filled baguettes seemed to be the favorite. Beautiful food all around me, complete with Technicolor smells.

I found an empty bench, of which there was no shortage of, and sat down just looking around with undisguised hunger. I felt famished; my stomach grumbled in protest at its enforced fast. I worked it out that it had been nearly a full week since I had last sat down to anything resembling a meal. Sure there had been snacks of bread….but then nothing for the last few days.

I watched as a passer-by stopped by a waste rubbish bin a few feet away from me, taking one last large bite out of his half eaten baguette; then drop the delicious looking meal into the open mouth of the bin, as if feeding it. He walked quickly away, the food already forgotten.

I was suddenly angry with him for such a hideous show of waste. Didn't he know that there were starving people in the world who'd give anything to have what he had just thrown away, so casually discarded like a one night stand?

A sudden shocking thought jumped into my head; why don't you grab the baguette from the bin and you'll not be hungry anymore!

I found myself glancing around to see who was looking at me, a reconnaissance of sorts. The grey bin was perhaps five feet away from me, two or three quick steps. All I'd have to do was reach in, swiftly as possible, and I would have something to eat.

I casually began to survey my surroundings to see who would spot my act of self-preservation.

A small group of female office workers sat opposite me, chattering away, nibbling at their food like well-dressed sparrows on a fence. A policeman was walking slowly along on his beat, lost in thought. Shoppers ambled along, clutching bags, and a gaggle of school kids on lunch break made lots of noise near a small shabby man selling papers who shouted all the louder for someone to buy his goods.

My heart was thumping at the thought of getting that baguette from the bin and I felt as though I was getting ready to rob a bank, I felt that nervous.

I took a deep, steadying breath, then was up on my feet and heading for the bin. Five feet, four feet, then three, glancing about as casually as I could manage, two feet, right hand poised to reach in and grab my food.....

.....And passing by the bin, my nerve deserting me as a small girl looked my way. I had been beaten away by the glance of a six-year-old girl in pigtails!

As I headed slowly away from the area a deep sludge-like sense of shame choked me at what I had so nearly done.

Eating from a rubbish bin!

Could things get any worse than that?

The answer that question was a resounding YES! They could get worse as I found out later that afternoon on my return to the rarefied air of the Consulate offices.

It was late afternoon by the time the same lady as I'd seen earlier could make time to interview me again. She looked like a doctor about to pass on a particularly nasty piece of news to a patient who considered himself healthy.

"I am afraid that there's nothing we can do to help you at this time", she paused, then added a softer," Sorry." And managed to sound as if she was sincere. Of that I had no doubt but it didn't help me in anyway. Best wishes never fed anyone yet.

I was close to tears, not a nice position to be in especially in front of a stranger, and a lady at that.

"What do I do?"

"Is there really no one who can help out with the coach fare back to

UK?"

"No one at all. I've told you that." I was sinking- fast. " I don't know what I'm going to do."

I stood up, feeling as if I was sleep walking and it was all a bad dream. All my hopes had been pinned on getting a little help from here, now all were dashed to the floor like broken pottery.

As I was leaving the building I heard the nice ladies voice behind me. She had followed me out and I hadn't been aware, wrapped up as I was in my thoughts. She handed me a small scrap of paper.

"Go to this address. They'll put you up for the night." She turned and was gone leaving me alone.

The address she had given me was for a men's homeless hostel, a forty-minute walk away. I found the place by simply showing the paper to passer-bye's, who in turn, pointed the way. I received a few contemptuous looks and was ignored more than once as I asked for help.

The building looked run down from the outside, an air of crumbling depression and despondency hanging over the place like an old mildewed blanket. I shuddered to think what it would be like on the inside.

As I rounded the corner, stepping onto the road leading to the hostel, I found that there was already a long queue of men standing outside, waiting for the double wooden doors to open. A low murmur of voices, like bees in a hive, reached across to me, and few drunks shouted now and then as if to keep order in the crowd.

I walked by on the opposite side of the road having a good look and I didn't like what I saw. Not one bit.

Most of the men were way older than I was and all were filthy to say the very least. The wind was blowing my way and I caught an unholy whiff of vomit, body odor and, the cherry on the cake, that boozy smell that only hard line drinkers exude. I could smell this hideous cocktail of humanity even above the fumes of passing traffic.

Several of the men had given up standing and had collapsed, or laid down, on the damp pavement, oblivious to those around them. Everyone simply stepped over them.

I checked the paper to make sure. This was the place, no doubt about that.

As I watched from a safe distance, a minor shuffle broke out, ending as quickly as it had begun as a bottle of something was offered and taken. Backs were slapped and life went on.

I walked to the end of the street and stood there, staring back at the queue and shuddered. What an awful place it was. No wonder the rich never mix with the poor.

A sense of horror rose up in me at the thought of going anywhere near that place and I decided that I'd rather sleep rough, just until …well, just until I didn't know what.

I turned and went in search of a hiding place for the night.

The best accommodations I could find for the night as darkness closed in was a large, well-kept park that would be rather nice in any other circumstances than the one I was in now.

I found a bench and sat there surveying my surroundings. A children's park was just behind me and I could make out the swings and slides and sand pits, now empty and rather sad looking.

Few people were about as night closed in, just those passing through the park as a short cut to get home to warm, comfortable houses and friendly family. As I sat there I felt like a man fallen overboard and no one to know I was in the water.

I found a covered place to sleep behind a building that I guessed was used by the park attendants and set about steeling myself for a night out in the open.

Then, to make matters worse, it began to rain, gentle and warm to begin, but soon it became a torrent and I was soaked through in a matter of minutes. A cold wind sprang up and added to the assault on me and I was soon thoroughly demoralized and shivering uncontrollably.

My thoughts turned to the hostel. "At least they'll be warm and dry." I had got into the habit of those who spent time alone and I often talked aloud to myself.

I lasted a few more minutes, holding out against the inevitable, then quickly packed up my sleeping bag, and began to make my way to the hostel, cold, soaked and right at the end of my tether.

As I walked along I had a strong feeling of dread made real as I paused outside the doors to the hostel. The queue had gone and everything looked normal on the street.

Taking a deep breath I stepped inside.

CHAPTER THIRTEEN

The formalities to enter the hostel were very simple and easy to follow, even for the dullest of applicants; you simply had to be brave enough to walk through the door and you had to look rough, a dress code of sorts. I was both brave enough and rough enough, now rain soaked as well, smelling slightly reminiscent of a dog back from a walk across wet fields. You know the kind of smell.

I gave my name to an elderly man just inside the doorway who appeared very surprised by spoken English. He called through for someone to interpret and I just stood there dripping wet, a small pool of water forming at my feet.

A rather large built, bald headed man turned up from within the depths of the hostel after a few minutes. He shook my hand." How can we help you?" he asked the very obvious but was smiling, a good sign. "My name is Claude." he added, his English passable.

"I have nowhere to stay," I fumbled for the wet, soggy scrap of paper with the hostels address on it, holding it out to him like an entry ticket to a club.

He took it and inspected the words." Ah, La Consulate." He nodded once as if the paper contained important information only he could see.

He spoke quickly, but gently, to the doorkeeper, who nodded and asked me my name. He wrote in a neat copper plate script and then placed a bold tick next to it.

"Follow me" Claude said, then paused at the door." Have you ever stayed in a hostel before?"

I shook my head, "No."

He sighed a deep, heartfelt sigh, a sad look on his face as he opened the door for me to step through.

"Then it will not be a pleasant experience for you. Come on!"

⊂►

If ever a man had told the truth it was Claude.

My first glimpse of the inside of the facility was exactly how I'd always imagine Hell to be. Awful beyond words.

The whole of the ground floor was one massive dormitory with low metal military type beds crammed in, side by side, and from wall to wall. There was no spare space so you had to walk crablike and sideways to move between beds.

The noise was instantly deafening and the sudden stench was like nothing I had ever experienced before; it was so bad that it felt as if I was ingesting it rather than smelling it, like a sudden fall into an open sewer with an open mouth.

A wave of nausea gripped me and for a few seconds I gagged and had to turn away. I looked back to the exit and seriously considered making a run for it, fresh air unexpectedly precious.

Claude watched me for a second, and then beckoned me to follow him, stepping past other 'residents' moving towards a far corner of the room where the stench was even more odious, if that was possible. In this little corner of France there were no windows or open doors to help the air circulate. It was if all the awfulness of the smells had collected here like sludge at the bottom of a slow moving toxic river.

Claude pointed to a lone bed, crammed in between two others, their occupants sitting there staring at me, sizing me up. I tried to ignore them.

"You are lucky." He said as he helped me make up the bed." This is the last one left."

The bed had a rubber bottom sheet, a pillow and two rough looking serge blankets. Claude looked pleased with himself as he finished helping me. "A place to sleep."

I set my small suitcase down at the foot of the bed and it sat there like an obedient dog not sure what to do.

At that moment in time I felt as though all life had come to a crashing end. Just being near the two men next to me on adjoining beds was enough to make me scratch. They were the filthiest couple of human beings I had ever seen, let alone be touching close. And I had to sleep only inches away from them!

Claude moved very close and whispered right into my ear, making it impossible for anyone to hear, even then I could barely make out what he said," You have any valuables on you or in your case?"

"No."

"Any money at all, or your passport, I suggest you give it to me to be locked away." he looked as serious as it was possible to be." Or else you will be robbed while you sleep and hurt. Bad." It was a statement of a fact and sent a shiver down my spine.

I managed a thin smile, "I can look after myself." But as I said the words I heard how hollow and unconvincing they were, even to my own ears.

Claude gave a very French shrug and walked off, shaking his head. I had a very strong feeling as I watched my only friend cross the hall that he'd heard that one before.

Some twenty minutes after my arrival there was a ripple of movement in the dorm as if some unheard and important signal had been given as men rose from beds and moved slowly to a set of double doors at one end of the dorm, forming a queue of sorts.

The doors opened and I had my first memorable sight of what was passed as a dining room for the hungry. It was feeding time at the zoo only this time you were allowed to feed the animals.

I sat on the edge of my bed, watching as the line shuffled along, the dorm quieter now. My stomach was grumbling as I waited for the lines to shorten. Then I had a sudden concern that it would all be gone by the time I finally reached the front, so I hurried over, my pride left back on the bed, alone and surprised.

I had no idea what was being served as the normal aroma of cooking food had been forced back at gunpoint by the disgusting odor in the dorm.

Already it felt that the smell was sticking to my very skin. I resisted the urge to scratch.

I joined the food line wondering what one earth was on the menu for tonight.

Dinner was a large bowl of meaty soup, two very thick slices of bread and the best mug of chicory coffee I had ever tasted in my life!

Long rows of wooden tables were jam-packed with men stuffing their faces with the food, some as fast as they could as though they were frightened that someone would steal the food out of their very mouths. Some glanced around as they ate, obviously nervous of a sudden thief taking their bread, or looking out for enemies.

Others were eating at a slower pace, as though savoring each and every mouthful, chewing the goodness out of every single morsel. Bowls were licked so hard I wondered if the pattern would come off as well.

Compared to meal times back in the Legion where loud, cheerful banter was the regular sound to be heard, I found the entire experience here a surreal episode in a whole series of undreamed of events. I never could've thought I'd ever sit at a table such as this.

On my table someone was violently sick into his bowl; but then carried on eating seconds later as if unaware of what he'd just done. No one seemed upset by what had happened in front of them, of someone eating his own vomit.

Others at the table were very obviously drunk. Some were noticeably mentally disturbed and a whole range of strange behavior was taking place as I spooned in my food. Someone near me a few places away suddenly screamed like a madman, hugely loud, but somehow it just fitted in perfectly with everything else going on. I soon came to the conclusion that the bizarre was the new normal.

I had thought that I had met some nasty looking men in the Legion; but there were a few here who positively scared the life out of me at first glance and I made a firm mental note to avoid these guys like the plague and to always keep my trusty knife very close to hand, ready to be used. Already I was acclimatizing to my new surroundings.

As I spooned in my soup I reflected that although I had been here in the hostel for less than one whole hour, it was as though I had been transported to a distant, more alien world, one I didn't like, many millions of miles from the earth and life I had been familiar with. The inhabitants of my new world were of a strain and form like I'd never seen.

127

After the meal had been served and devoured right down to the last crumb, Claude sought me out to explain the hostels routine, basic as it was. Induction each evening was always followed by dinner, then showers were offered to those who wished to have a wash down. A mug of coffee was served just before lights out with some bread if available. Alcohol was strictly prohibited as was drugs of any kind, except medication. Lights out until breakfast at 7am to 7.45am, then everybody had to vacate the building until 6pm when the process would start all over again, seven days a week, all year round. A simple routine but one that was a life support system to many men.

Did I understand the routine? I nodded politely. It wasn't rocket science.

I was beginning to like this guy, Claude, and his ready smile to all he talked to. He didn't seem to be fazed by the condition many were in and I could see that this was responded too with a kind of trust. No one was going to bite the hand that fed them. Besides, Claude looked as if he could handle anything.

I was informed that the hostel was a joint venture by the local administration and groups of concerned local citizens, including church groups and was staffed by volunteers. No one was paid and all who worked here, night after night, did it all for love and not for money, out of a real and genuine concern for those in dire need. Those who helped were mainly older folks and I wondered where the young ones were.

I speculated what drove a normal, comfortable person to enter such a place as this and suffer the smells and sights to help total strangers. Compassion wasn't in my vocabulary yet. What I saw here was love in action and it was the first time I'd come across it.

Local bakeries supplied left over bread and pastries. Other shops handed over meats and vegetables and the daily menu depended solely on what others didn't need. But there was always something to eat and that was what mattered.

If the evening soup was thick then there had been an abundance of charity. When the soup was wafer thin, well, at least it would be warm and there was always bread in some form or another.

Claude left me alone sitting on my bed and it was reasonably quite as many men had gone off to shower, a slightly pointless act as filthy clothes went straight back on, but it was nice to have the option. Not tonight, I decided, as much as my skin crawled with greasy filth. I felt very vulnerable and wanted to be careful to begin with and see whom the ones to watch out for were.

The dining room had been transformed into an entertainment area when an ancient TV set had been wheeled in on a school type trolley with much cheering from the inmates. It was the only frivolity that I had seen or heard since my arrival and brought a little touch of humanity to this desolate place. Even the homeless loved the soaps.

Already in the dorm was that particularly irritating sound of someone snoring, a noise I hate to this very day, as some just fell asleep, fully clothed where they lay.

For some time I just sat there watching the tidal ebb and flow of this group of human rubbish, ones discarded by polite society. As lights out approached I began to feel an incredible loathing towards the other men in the room, especially those nearest me, so close that if I turned over I would touch the bed next to me. Sardines had more space than I had and it was impossible to ignore the closeness of others, something I hated with a passion.

One guy spoke to me and I swore back at him, deliberately injecting as much aggression as I could muster into my voice, which wasn't hard at that point. He backed instantly away, hands raised in supplication, knowing violence was very close at hand and that he would be the target of my fury. He also noticed my knife.

Those nearby looked away, quickly blind and deaf, not willing to get involved. They survived life on the streets by keeping their heads down when trouble reared its ugly unforgiving serpent's teeth, and by putting on the cloak of invisibility that the homeless wear as they move among everyday life. It was if they lived in a parallel world, unseen and unheard.

Even after the main dorm lights had been turned off there was more than enough to see by as the fire escape lights flickered on, as if even darkness was afraid to safely come in the hostel and stay the night.

The noises of the night had somehow fuelled the earlier loathing I had felt into something more; an almost incandescent anger at these useless, drunken, drug-taking, pathetic, excrement covered pieces of human rubbish that surrounded me as far as the nose could smell.

How could anyone let themselves go to get into such a state as these men had?

Where was their self-respect and dignity? How had they turned into such creatures so vile that they had to live and sleep like this?

They were filthy, smelt vile and had given up on life, sinking to the bottom of the heap, and then going one step further; here.

I was so furious that I was right on the point of lashing out violently against those nearest to me that and I stood up, right on the edge of cracking up and kicking off big time.

Then a sudden ice cold thought leapt into mind as hard and clinical as bad news from a policeman on your doorstep.

I was here, tonight, with these men and no matter how hard I tried to put it off I came to realize something so terrible I nearly stopped breathing.

I was no different from any of these men. I had become the very thing I loathed.

The enormity of it all broke through and I just stood there and wept and wept, not caring who heard me.

That night was without a doubt, the worst in my entire life, before or since.

For long hours on end it seemed as if I struggled with my very sanity, and there was a feel of unseen yet powerful hands belonging to some malevolent force that was endeavoring to pull me over the edge of some eternally deep abyss from which there could be no return.

As I sat in the semi darkness it seemed as if there was a sinister blackness beyond lack of light that was pressing in on me in an intelligent and purposeful way. As if it meant me harm.

I was scared beyond words.

The night sounds did nothing to help me as some cried out in terror as nightmares invaded their dreams like violent burglars.

Others talked to long-ago friends, possibly family, calling to them by name; maybe veiled memories of happier times, gone forever, never to be repeated again.

And somewhere, at the far end of the room, a man was being raped many times over.

Morning seemed as impossible to reach as a man trapped by flames behind pad-locked doors struggling to get to an open window and live to tell the tale. I waited and hoped to make it.

Somewhere during the ordeal of the long night I must have drifted off into a fitful sleep waking with a jolt at the sounds of someone kick starting their lungs with a bout of hideous coughing, similar to a diesel engine on a cold winter's morning.

A surge of relief that I had made it through the night gripped me and I even managed a grin at the man lying next to me. Not surprisingly he didn't return the effort, no doubt remembering my outburst last night. But who cared about what he thought? I was alive and kicking and in one piece.

Breakfast was a simple and quick affair; coffee and last night's left over bread by now hard and nearly stale, but very welcome all the same. A hole was filled and I pocketed a large chunk for later.

By 7.30am the hostel was emptying itself, vomiting out the inhabitants from its intestines; it was like an exodus of the helpless and hopeless, men wandering away to fill the time until the hostel opened it wide mouth once again. I vaguely wondered what the professionally homeless did all day.

I had arranged with Claude, who worked full time with a local church, to leave my suitcase in the locked staff room, as I didn't fancy lugging it around with me all.

Outside the air was clean and fresh and I took in several huge lungful's of free air hoping it would clean out whatever may have of got in, any germs or bugs in the stench of the 'black hole', as I had dubbed the dormitory.

My priority was to get home, the how was a major problem. So I found a comfortable spot to sit down near the River Garonne close to a large bridge and began to think things through. I made a mental inventory of my state of affairs as it was in the present day.

I was not hungry; one up from this time yesterday, and even had a chunk of bread in my pocket. Good so far.

I had a place to stay, as a last resort, if nothing happened at the Consulate. It wasn't the Ritz Hotel and my skin crawled involuntarily at the prospect of a second night in the Hostel, but it was a roof over my head.

So …a plan was needed and fast.

I had always found that I think well when I walk, so off I went for a planning meeting for one.

><>

Within ten minutes I had come up with PLAN A.

Simply put I would visit the consulate each and every day and keep asking for help until they got so fed up with me pestering them that they would give in and help in some way.

It was now Tuesday and I had only a few days until the weekend when they would no doubt be shut.

As part of PLAN A, I would also try to find some casual work of any nature to get a few francs to help towards the cost of the ticket back to the UK. I was sure that if the consulate saw I was trying then they would help out as well.

This was PLAN A.

There was no PLAN B.

Feeling slightly more positive and buoyant of mood I made my way to the consulate, last night a distant horrific memory, one I pushed away from my mind like an annoying drunk at a private party.

And to top things off, the sun was shining for once.

$$\rightarrowtail\!\!\bigcirc$$

By Thursday I was down to PLAN W and could feel all hope evaporating of ever getting home.

I had gone to many local businesses to try and get work, any work, but because of my lack of French language, I was sent packing. All I wanted was simple cash in hand jobs, not long term roles with a pension and holiday pay.

The prejudice in people was so obvious as soon as I approached them. I have to admit that my appearance wasn't Guards Division smart as I hadn't washed or shaved for now nearly two weeks. A rather nasty smell followed me about that appalled even me when I caught a whiff of myself. The streets were changing me and not for the better.

I can't blame those I asked for work for rejecting me but it was hard to be judged so fast, so often, by people who had no idea who you were and what you wanted to do.

You imagine any street person you have ever seen, just pick one now, and then imagine that person entering your work place and asking for a job.

I stood no chance of getting anywhere and I was right on the point of giving up.

$$\rightarrowtail\!\!\bigcirc$$

The Consulate staff and I were on first name terms by now as I turned up morning and afternoon, a professional smile fixed to my face. I was determined to be nice so as not to give them the chance to ban me.

But the answer each time I visited them was the exact same. "Sorry,

Mr. Moore, we can't help you at this time. Is there anyone who can help you?"

By Thursday afternoon I was feeling very low and just nodded my reply and walked out when I received the standard reply. I was through with the jockey banter and false cheerfulness that I had been giving out. My reserve of pleasantness was just about gone.

Thursday night back in the hostel was as bad as it was possible to get. Several fights broke out, suddenly and for no discernable reason and ended with one man being seriously stabbed, needing urgent medical help.

The ambulance staff would only enter the hostel when the police arrived and so there was a delay of several minutes before he could be helped. I never knew what happened to him after he was carried away.

The attacker was known to all but no one talked, as was the way of things. The police met a wall of very loud silence.

The attacker was a brute of a man and everyone who was sane was scared of him, deferring to him as he strutted around that night, full of what he had done, knowing that he was the undisputed champion of the world of the hostel.

At one stage he came over to my corner of the dorm demanding cigarettes from those who had them, getting what he wanted. He helped himself to whatever he desired.

He said something to me and I ignored him, but he stepped over the beds as if launching an attack at me, his voice raised and eyes wild; until he saw my knife and knew that I would cut him if he came any closer. I told him to back off, or words to that effect, and there was a tense standoff for what seemed like minutes as we faced up, ready for anything.

Despite the language barrier he had understood perfectly what I was about and withdrew, making a big show and shouting as loud as he could so that everyone could hear what he intended to do to me. He demonstrated by drawing his own knife across his throat in an unmistakable cutting motion. At that point I was a man marked down for death and he didn't look like a man to forget a grudge.

Until lights out he sat on his bed, a scant thirty feet away, just staring, as if waiting for the chance to get back at me.

I knew there would be little sleep that night.

Friday afternoon and I was seated in the consulate waiting room, hoping to see someone; but despite a serious lack of visitors to the office, no one could find the time to see me today.

I knew that I was becoming an annoyance and embarrassment to the staff and it now showed in their faces. Gone now were the professional looks and the real person was getting through. I have never held anything against these people, as they had to work within the systems rules.

As I watched the office staff work behind the security screen, studiously ignoring me, I became agitated by their apparent lack of concern for me, a fellow Brit and more to the point, a person in real need. I was being treated badly just when I needed a little bit of help.

At closing time I still hadn't been seen and was asked to leave.

As I stood to go and I turned and asked in a very loud voice, making sure that everyone could hear me.

"Can I ask one last question?"

The staff nodded collectively.

"If I die will my body be taken home?"

There was a shocked silence as I turned and left heading down the long stairs and out in the open streets, not caring what anyone thought.

Without a doubt I now knew for sure that I wouldn't get any help from the consulate, so I needed to get some cash and fast.

That left two options as far as I could see.

One. I could lay in wait and mug someone as they passed by and get the cash that way.

Two. I could do what I had seen others from the hostel do as I had walked about Bordeaux. I could beg for money.

Two choices and neither of them ideal.

That Friday night during those long unending hours of the trial by hostel, I wrestled with my decision between the choices I had to make. I had no option, it had to be one or the other if I was to get cash and get home. Desperate times called for desperate measures.

I had a knife and wasn't afraid in the slightest to use it in the right circumstances but there was still just enough decency in me to shy away from attacking an innocent person, no matter my need.

How long this trace of humanity would last in me was anyone's guess, but it was slowly leaking away, like oxygen from a holed spaceship.

So, my mind was made up, my decision firm. On Saturday morning, in just a few hours from now, I Gary Wayne Moore, formerly of the Corps of

RMP and late of the Foreign Legion, would go begging on the streets of Bordeaux.

My decision finally complete, it seemed as though sleep was disgusted with what I had planned and left me alone, wide awake and with nothing but thoughts of what was to come.

It didn't make for a pleasant time.

><

CHAPTER FOURTEEN.

Saturday was a turning point in my life as I hit a new rock bottom; plummeting to depths I never dreamed was possible, as dignity became a luxury I couldn't afford. The poor, it seemed, were always bankrupt of hope.

As I stood at various locations, always where crowds gathered, such as shopping centers, I simply asked complete strangers for money as they came past. I had learned a few simple phrases of begging French to make me appear more professional.

In any town or city you visit anywhere in the world you will always without a shadow of doubt come across beggars. Next time you see one, then you will have seen exactly how I was at that time, the person I had somehow become.

For hours on end I stood, smiling and very polite, my hand out for any coin that could be spared, but amazingly, I had become completely invisible to the naked eye as thousands walked past me and never saw a thing. I had the impression that if I had been on the ground in front of them then just stepping over me would've be fine for them. As long as no one had to acknowledge that I was there. I was a non-person.

Two people stick out in my mind from that Saturday over twenty five years later as I sit and write this account, as though these particular individuals have been branded on some part of my brain forever, unable to be erased.

The first was a well-dressed middle-aged man who stopped right in front of me, the crowds of shoppers swirling past us like we were two rocks in the middle of a fast moving river.

He stood there and began to shout and yell at me for no other reason than that I'd just held out my hand as he had passed. He yelled loudly, drawing attention from the crowds. I had no idea what he was saying, but I got the gist of the body of the text. Anger stained his face and I had no idea why he got as upset as he did, right on the verge of striking me.

As he left he spat at me, a great big greeny that narrowly missed and stuck to a low wall just behind me.

The second person I will never forget was a young girl, maybe 15 years or so, who stopped and spoke with me. She was a kind faced girl with long brown hair, who had little English so conversation was brief. Sign language took over and she made an eating motion, which I took to mean, "Are you hungry?"

I nodded, wondering how much she would give me. The day had been a poor introduction to my new profession and I only had a few miserable coppers for all the hours I had spent degrading myself in a very public way.

The girl smiled and walked off into a bakers shop just a few yards away. I had been eying up some of the cakes and baguettes in the window earlier, my mouth watering, unable to even pay for a crumb of the wonders behind the glass.

She came out minutes later with a small white bag, which she handed over to me with a nice friendly smile. Inside was a small meat pie and I could feel its warmth through the thin paper against the chill of the day. The smell was divine.

I had a flash of disappointment, as it was cash that I had been hoping for, to get my ticket home and not a silly little meat pie that I could swallow whole in one go.

Then the girl smiled and said, "My last money. I have to walk home now. No bus," then she patted my arm like a smaller, happier sister, then turned and left me, stunned by her random act of kindness. She had used her bus fare home to feed me. I felt a sudden lump in my throat, amazed at what she had done.

As I watched her walk through the crowds until I lost sight of her, I realized that this was perhaps the greatest act of kindness that anyone had ever shown me, spending her last cash on a pie for a complete stranger, a waster like me.

Sometimes you have to buy them a pie.

I have never tasted a more delicious meat pie since that day and probably never will!

Monday morning was a wet, dark day with rain driving down in solid sheets of cold water. Within minutes of leaving the hostel I was soaked right through with little prospect of getting dry until I could get back into the hostels now familiar and welcome embrace. Hostel rules were rigid and no matter the weather the building had to be cleared during the day with no exceptions. I wondered where all the other men went too on days like this. I bet the library was full that day.

I found an empty doorway to a shop that had been closed down and boarded up. I was shivering already and had noticed that I was feeling the cold badly of late. The consulate didn't open until 9.30am, ages yet, so I just stood there stamping my feet to keep them warm, but failing miserably as the heat drained away through my soaking wet shoes.

Over the weekends begging I had managed to collect the grand total of seven French Francs, a pitiful amount to show for what I had been doing.

I decided that begging wasn't going to pay for anything so I had made up my mind that I would indeed turn to robbery, possibly later that night when it was dark.

Desperate times call for desperate acts.

And I was getting desperate.

I was second in line for when the consulate doors open, just behind a tubby man in a black business suit. He looked me up and down in a rather superior way, like some officer inspecting his troops, then sniffed in disdain, turning away.

I grinned at him, getting right in his face, not willing to take any nonsense and said, "Morning, fat boy!"

He looked away embarrassed. I have always worked on the principle that if you can't take it, then don't give it.

Once inside and into the very familiar office I asked to see someone about my case and got the usual, "Take a seat and someone will see you soon."

So I sat and made myself as comfortable as I could despite being wet through and settled down to begin the waiting game. This time I didn't mind because outside, I could hear a storm blowing and here I was warm.

"Take your time." I said.

Twenty minutes later I was seated opposite the same middle-aged lady I had been dealing with on most of my visits. I don't remember her name but she was pleasant and likeable.

"Gary, nothing has changed since Friday," was her opening line, looking appropriately apologetic.

"Ah, but things have!" I proudly pulled out my entire fortune of seven Francs and piled the coins in the center of the table between us. I counted the coins out.

"Seven Francs." She observed, clearly a university graduate.

"Yeah." I pushed the coins across to her and she look surprised by the move." It's my down payment for my ticket home."

She looked even more surprised by this and managed a soft, "Oh." She composed herself and managed to say," How did you get this money?"

"I spent Saturday and Sunday begging." I looked her straight in the eyes." I have never asked anyone for anything in my life," I stammered over the words, like trying to sing with a mouthful of food. I was instantly on the verge of tears. "Can't you see that genuinely need your help? Please."

I'm not ashamed to say that tears did spill down my cheeks as the stress and strain of the last weeks threatened to break the dam of self-control that I was barely sustaining.

Sure I was a tough guy, able to hold my own; but now I was just trying to do the right thing and make amends.

I heard the door open, then shut softly as the lady left, leaving only her scent of lavender behind and a muttered," I'll be back in a tick," over her shoulder.

"God, help me."

This was the second time I'd spoken to Him.

$\gtrless \bigcirc$

And it was the second time that He answered me.

Ten minutes later the lady came back into the room, a half smile plastered all over her face. She pushed the pile of centimes and francs back to me." Put those in your pocket. I've just booked you a coach ticket home to Norwich for this Wednesday. I believe you are a genuine case and therefore we will help you this time." Then added, "Don't make a habit of this."

I could hardly believe my ears and sat open mouthed.

"You will, of course, have to pay us back as the money has come out of our emergency fund, which is limited." She pushed a form over, which I signed, then gave another with the address of the travel agent on where I had to collect the ticket.

She stood to show our meeting was over, suddenly businesslike, and shook my hand.

"Gary, get your bloody life sorted out."

"I will. That's a promise."

$\gtrless \bigcirc$

Wednesday soon came and I made a special effort that morning, rising early to have a cold shower, in the hope that I wouldn't smell too much on the coach journey, first to Paris, then onto London, finally Norwich.

I had a few clean clothes in my suitcase and I used these, stuffing my others away.

I took breakfast as usual, and realized with a start that I hadn't taken any notice of the awful smell that had made me feel so ill on arrival. I was also on nodding terms with some of the guys and had even picked up a little pidgin French to get me by in here. It just went to prove that even the worst of places could become normal, given enough time, as you adapted and changed like a transplanted plant from field to pot.

Claude took me to one side as I prepared to leave. He had been overjoyed the day when I had told him I was going home. In fact he had nearly hugged me.

In his small office he gave me 20 francs, a small fortune, to buy food for the journey and said he hoped God would bless me in my life.

Maybe one day I'll meet up with Claude again and I will thank him for all he did for me and the others there. I have a feeling he was a true Christian believer by his actions alone and the compassion that exuded from him like an expensive after-shave. He wore Jesus well.

Departure time came and I was pleasantly surprised to find that the coach was only a quarter full and so I was able to have two seats to spread out on. In fact during the entire journey back to Norwich I never once had anyone next to me.

I had some bread, cheese and a couple of bottles of water and as the coach pulled out of Bordeaux I felt an excitement that whatever was going to happen next was definitely better than what I had just been through.

Also I had a few questions about this God and wondered where on earth I could find some answers.

><

CHAPTER FIFTEEN

The journey home was more than comfortable and as I sat there on the coach as it travelled first across France, then England, I had long empty hours to ponder what on earth I was going to do when I finally made it back. Now reality was here and happening I found it rather scary to be honest.

I knew for a certainty that I wasn't going to be welcomed home with open friendly arms, of that I was under no false illusions. After my lies and outrageous behavior I would be more than surprised if they wanted to even see me in the street, let alone talk to and help me.

I toyed with the idea of asking Mum to put me up for a few nights; or maybe even asking my Granny, in Beccles. For long hours I chewed things over, like a tough toffee stuck in my teeth, of just what I should do, but solid conclusions didn't materialize no matter how hard I tried to reason things through.

Whatever I decided to do, one thing was for certain and that was that I would need transport to get about. On the National Express coach from London to Norwich I cut short the trip and got off at the market town of Thetford. I had lived there as a teenager and my sister, Debbie, still lived there in a nice little flat.

Before leaving for the Legion I had left her my old yellow Ford Cortina to do with as she pleased. I had said to sell it for extra cash or keep it and learn to drive. It had been taxed and MOT'd, and I hoped, as I made my way from the bus station next to Button Island in the town Centre that she had kept it.

I found her flat and to my relief the car was still parked where I had left it. A good start. I hoped that it would actually start, as it hadn't been moved in a while.

Debbie was in and I gave her a story, reverting back instantly into my old ways, embellishing the truth about where I had been and what I had done, and that I desperately had to have my car back. I also borrowed five pounds, promising to give it back in a few days' time. Lies tripped off my tongue as easily as a priest's prayer.

She was fine about things and I was soon back behind the wheel of my car, feeling like the master of the universe as I drove along, music blasting out as I headed along the A11 and Norwich.

The petrol tank was nearly full and I had bought a pack of six Mars Bars, my favorite food of all time. I found it hard to believe that just a few days ago I was begging in a foreign country, surviving in a hostel full of drunk's, druggies and madmen, and I marveled at how life had turned around so quick.

Already I had forgotten about my two fast-track prayers, but God hadn't forgotten about me.

Bowthorpe is a large housing estate on the outskirts of Norwich, Norfolk, and is a mixture of private accommodation, council and housing association homes that even today is growing outwards with new developments springing up all the time.

Mum and Bob were buying a three bed roomed house on Styleman road right in the middle of the estate. I knew the house well having helped them with the move from Thetford.

I drove slowly past the house, like a gunman checking to see if his intended target-to-be was at home. The front room curtains were open and as I rolled by I could see Mum and my younger brother, Darren, moving about inside. Mum was drinking from a cup as she talked to Darren about something.

The scene was so normal looking and every day and one seen a million times before. But to be honest, I had never expected to see them again as my trip to join the Legion was designed to be as final as the loss of a limb. I vividly remember making the decision to leave for the Legion and making the resolution to forget totally about my family, as if they had never existed at all, like a file deletion, lost forever.

I parked round the corner, suddenly very scared about driving up, knocking on the door and saying, "Hi Mum, it's me! Any chance of a cuppa?" After all I had been through of late, of facing terrors I had never been aware ever existed, I discovered that this was what frightened me the most. To face up to my wrongs.

I drove round the block and made a second pass and this time the curtains had been drawn tightly shut, as if they had got sudden word that I was about and had closed them as a sign for me to keep way, a way to protect themselves from a predator.

My courage deserted me and I decided to drive to Beccles and speak to my Granny. I hoped that the 30-minute drive would somehow enable me to by some means find the bravery that I had lacked here.

Full of a fool's confidence of climbing a mountain with a frayed rope, I pulled away.

The very same scene enacted itself at Beccles as the shame of what I had done and the way that I had treated Granny hit home in an almost physical way. As I drove by 23 Common lane a lifetime of good and happy memories from childhood swept in on me like a breaking tsunami wave, as if to remind me of how far I had fallen from grace. Just about every happy time I'd had took place with Granny and Granddad in that house and gardens. Now I couldn't even walk in through the side gate.

I was a self-infected leper.

Shame is a nasty emotion to feel and is nearly impossible to explain to someone who had never experienced it. I can't think of anything to compare shame with.

I sat outside Granny's house for quite a while, alone in the dark, hoping against hope that Granny would look outside, see me in the car, and then call me in so I could tell her how sorry I was for all I had done. But it was now late and she would be in bed, asleep. I could picture her room. In my mind's eye I walked softly through the house I loved so much.

Maybe I should just get out and knock on the door but my courage and good intentions had both deserted me, as if unwilling to sit in the car with me, leaving behind an ashamed coward.

All the good and noble reasons for trying to get back home that had carried me through the recent trials in France had drained away, chased away by fear, leaving only that bitter taste of failure that now stuck to the roof of my mouth like old cabbage.

I drove up to the common land at the end of the road where the golf course was and parked up in the total darkness that matched exactly how I feeling. As I sat there in the silence it was if all the ghosts of happier times came to taunt me through the long cold hours of the night, a kaleidoscope of images, complete with sound that paraded around me until a kind of uneasy sleep mercifully pulled me under.

I was back home but now I wished I wasn't.

By the time dawn decided to make an appearance I was stiff, cold and thoroughly tired. It had been a tough night to get through, although not as bad as some I had survived of late.

I had eaten all the Mars Bars and was feeling slightly sick at so much chocolate in one sitting.

It had been a bitterly cold night, with an east wind that had tried to eat its way through the shell of the car to get at me. I had kept starting the engine to try and keep warm. It had worked but at the expense of using up a quarter of a tank of fuel, a newly precious commodity as I had no cash to buy more.

So- option time

Mum was out for now.

Granny was also a non-runner.

Immediate needs?

Cash, as always but now not just for food but also for fuel for the car, which doubled as a kind of mobile home.

I knew it would be fairly easy to get a full time job in a factory, weekly paid, and I could always sleep rough in the car to begin with. Not ideal but a much better deal than the hostel back in France. I shuddered at the thought of that place.

If I found work then I would still need some cash for the first week until I got paid on the second week, as most places required you to work one week in hand.

There wasn't anyone to borrow money from. I got out of the car, stretched and began walking, thinking about the solution. The common ground was a place I had spent many hours on as a small child. There was a play park that had the biggest slide I had ever seen, until I went back as an adult and saw how small it really was!

A pathway circles the common land with a golf course of sorts in the middle section. There was also an old world war two machine gun concrete pillbox still waiting for the German invasion right in the heart of the common land and I had spent countless hours as a pretend soldier storming the concrete building and being a hero.

As I walked slowly along I had a sudden idea.

Why not sign on as unemployed? Our social security system was and is very good and surely I qualified?

I seemed to remember someone telling me once that if you were homeless as well as unemployed then they could make over the counter payments from the social security offices, and in cash, to get over the problem of not having a fixed abode. How true this was I had no idea but it was worth checking out.

Well I was most certainly homeless and out of work as well. Living in a car must qualify?

They had to help someone like me.

With a spring in my step and the cold forgotten I hurried back to the car and a trip back to Norwich.

The Department of Health and Social Security (DHSS) had its main office in a rather unflattering concrete building in the red light district of the city, an area grandly named Mountergate. The DHSS office also had an impressive name, Baltic House, and some said that the welcome you received there was as winter cold as the northern European sea with waters that lap the shores of Sweden, Poland, Lithuania and Latvia, that the building was named after. It certainly looked like an old KGB building.

The system in the building was simple. Inside the double front doors was a ticket machine with black printed numbers on a paper roll. You tore off a ticket and, clutching it tightly, you found a seat on one of those Government Issue plastic seats that made your bottom sweat after five minutes. Here you waited and waited until your number was displayed on a large orange digital display, the sort you found at tennis matches.

It was a simple and effective system and even the dullest claimants understood how it all worked.

The large waiting room was nearly empty, the morning rush over as the desperate and those urgently requiring help had got in first thing, not that it really mattered here as the staff worked at their own pace and speed, doing the best they could inside a system that was creaking with ineffectiveness even then.

Six others were waiting their turn to be summoned to the glass partition that separated claimants from the claim handlers. The glass had been added to protect the office personnel, as there had been a long history of violent attacks on staff as frustrations had erupted into some very nasty assaults. The DHSS was not a place to come for sympathy and it sometimes seemed cold and callous in its dealings with those at the lower end of the social scale.

I grabbed a ticket as I walked in, number 24, and picked a seat well away from the other six folks there and began to wait my turn.

No magazines to read, no papers. Just sit and wait and listen to what the poor person at the one window that was open was trying to say through the glass partition. A small grill at the bottom of the dividing wall allowed loud speech and documents to pass through each way, a Berlin wall of sorts.

But you had to speak very loudly and therefore your private business became public knowledge, more so when it was empty of the usual crowds in the early morning sessions.

To pass the time I inspected the room and the other people there. Within two minutes I was bored of that. I tried to turn my brain off.

A few minutes later that present claimant finished and left the room, the twin entry doors screeching open, then slamming shut in a way that made my teeth set on edge. There was no mistaking that door and I wondered if the real reason for the glass partition was to keep that awful noise out.

The number changed on the board, and number 18 was called forward. A single mother, tiny newborn baby in buggy moved into the hot seat and began her interrogation.

I was beginning to feel the effects of the almost sleepless and cold night in my car and yawned and stretched…

…. And nearly jumped right out of my skin!

A large grey haired man was seated just two spaces away from me and I hadn't heard or seen anyone come through those noisy doors, or even walk down the aisle to get near me. I had only yawned for a few seconds, closed my eyes for even less.

It was as though he'd just appeared there and I had a sudden, unannounced flash back to the way the car had just appeared back in France, the one that had taken me right to the very steps of the Consulate. That had been silent as well.

The man nodded a greeting to me, which, unusually for me, I returned. Something was very odd here.

"Slow here, aren't they." He said, more a statement than a question. "Still, their hearts are in the right place."

"Yeah." I grunted. I didn't want to walk to anyone and was annoyed that he had chosen me to pester, with all the empty seats to pick from. I decided to ignore him as best I could. If he carried on then I would be very rude and maybe then he would get the hint.

Mum and baby finished and someone else filled the hot seat. One step closer to my turn.

"I've been staying at the YMCA." The man said matter -of –factually, as if continuing a conversation with me that I had been unaware of.

I decided to blank him out, not even giving him the impression that I had even heard what he had just said to me. I was aware that he was staring directly at me. I didn't want to make nice talk and meet a new friend. He would get the point shortly, one way or another, of that I was confident.

"I'm leaving there today so there's a room spare for you, if you'll ask them for it." He paused but he now had my sudden complete attention." You will also hear about Gods love for you, Gary."

I was shocked that he even knew my name and that I needed a place to live. I sat there open mouthed, trying to find something to say but words seemed to be on strike, refusing to work for me.

He grinned at me and then nodded towards the number board." Your turn, I believe."

I looked at the numbers and it was number 24!

"How did you…"? I began but he waved me forward and I just got up and headed towards the glass wall and my appointment to begin my claim, totally stunned.

What was going on here? A stranger who appears and knows my homelessness and even knows my ticket number and knows my name?

As I sat down on yet another plastic seat at the partition I glanced quickly back and found that where I had been sitting with the man only seconds before, there were only empty seats!

He'd gone as fast and as silent as he had arrived.

What was going on here?

Looking back it was obvious that angels come in various shapes and sizes.

⟞⟨⟩

The interview to sign on as unemployed and homeless was easier than I had expected, the lady helpful and quick to tell me my rights on what I could and couldn't claim for. After the coldness of the consulates dealings with me, the DHSS was a walk in the park, a five star experience.

The lady filled in all the forms for me and all I had to do was to sign at the bottom of the thick application document. I was told to return that afternoon to receive an emergency over the counter payment for food needs.

The lady seemed genuinely surprised when I thanked her for her kind help she'd shown me, and gave me a lovely smile in return. I wonder if this was a first for her.

Being polite to someone you wanted help from is a sensible path to follow, especially when they hold all the cards.

With a few hours to spare in Norwich before I could collect my cash I decided to have a wander around. I still had the grand sum of 50pence in my pocket and headed off to the market place and the chip stalls there that served up the best fried chips on planet earth!

I had a feeling things were on the up for me.

⟞⟨⟩

The market place in Norwich is the focal point of the city and is opposite the city hall. Made up of dozens of colorfully roofed stalls it was the best place to get fresh meats, vegetables, fruits and cheap but good clothing. In fact you could get just about anything you needed from some corner of the market.

The fish and chip stalls were my favorite and the food came piping hot and wrapped in newspaper. I bought my chips, added plenty of salt and vinegar and went up into the memorial gardens, right above the market, which also housed the war memorial to the dead of the two world wars.

All the concrete seats were taken already so I found a corner of a wall and sat down and munched away happily. I was feeling very relaxed, a rare event for me. Pigeons flew everywhere, like excited children at a birthday party, knowing full well that the silly humans would toss them bits of chips and bread rolls if they flew close enough, or walked about on the concrete, making 'coo-ing' noises. It seemed to work well for them, as you didn't see many skinny birds.

I checked the time on the tall city hall clock, which was working for once and found that I still had 90 minutes before I had to get back to the DHSS and get some cash.

Finishing my chips I licked my fingers then tossed the bag into a bin and began walking. My thoughts turned to the man back in the DHSS earlier, and to be honest, it had shaken me up a bit. How he seemed to know things about me, like he had some divine insider knowledge of my life and situations. It was a bit spooky.

The words he had spoken, 'There's a spare room for you, if you ask them for it.' Kept playing inside my head, as if stuck there until acted upon.

A spare room? I could use a place to stay, as the thought of spending a second night sleeping in my Cortina really didn't appeal to me.

I knew the YMCA building was up on St. Giles street just a few minutes' walk away from the market place. I'd passed the place many times but had never had a reason to go inside. I didn't know anything about the place except that it was a Christian type of place where the God bashers met and the words stood for the ' Young Men's Christian Association. '

For want of something better to do and to kill some time I decided to wander up the road and have a look at the place.

It couldn't hurt to have a look, could it?

I did my usual thing and had a walk past to have a quick look, taking in the twin white door pillars, the clean entry doorway with the red, black and white triangle with the words YMCA within above the doorway and a reception desk of some kind set back inside.

It seemed safe so I turned back and stepped inside, not realizing that my life was about to be changed forever.

The reception desk had a sliding glass panel and two men sat there, drinking coffee and turned and faced as I walked in.

I later learned that they were Ron and Collin.

"Can I help you?" Ron asked pleasantly.

"I was told that you have a spare room here as someone's leaving.

How do I get it?" I was straight to the point, no small talk. A simple yes or no would do for me.

"Ok, first things first," said Ron as he hunted around on the desk for a form, then a pen, moving his swivel chair closer to the window. "I just need a few details, then I'll check with the residence manager to see what we have available."

As he asked questions I answered. I could see that the other guy with him, Collin, was looking a little apprehensive and kept glancing sideways at me, as if worried I would do something.

Certainly I was a rough looking character at that point. I still had a Legion skinhead; a growth of beard, shabbily dressed and I knew just how bad I smelt. I'd also developed a hard nasty stare which spelt out,' don't mess with me, or else!'

To give Ron Day his credit he didn't give away how much I must have of smelt or looked.

Looking back it was hardly surprising that I was intimidating to those I came across. My language was foul with every other word the 'F' bomb, even now when I was answering these questions being asked so kindly by Ron.

Ron finished the short form, made a low voice telephone call, and then turned back to me. He had a ready smile and I found myself warming to this guy, a rare occurrence for me.

He stood and faced me." Right then, Gary, if you can come back here in about one hour, we'll have a decision for then, OK?" he sounded sincere to me, no trace of bull in his voice.

I simply shrugged, "yeah, right." And then left without another word, already resolved that I would be spending another night in the car, my home for the foreseeable future.

What I didn't know until much, much later, was that the reason they put me on hold was that they were so very concerned by my appearance and character and my obviously violent nature that they, as Christians on the frontlines, needed to seek their God and see what He had to say about it all.

And speak He did and very clearly to everyone involved in the decision making process who prayed that day about me.

God said, *"Let this man in."* and so they did.

One hour later, almost to the minute, I found myself back at the

YMCA, unsure as to how and why I had come back.

This time I was taken through the locked security doors and into the main body of the building, past a snooker table and into the Residence Managers office, a tall guy called Norman Littler, who was as laid back as it came. I found his northern accent quite soothing as he spoke with me.

A short interview took place, checking details on the form and I explained events as they had taken place over the last months and weeks, including the Legion.

If Norman was surprised or shocked by my story it didn't show. He certainly wasn't impressed and for some reason, that impressed me. I was being treated without prejudice and that was a rare as rocking horse teeth.

It was explained to me that the 'Y' was a Christian organization and did I have any faith, just in case I died and had to be buried. Norman laughed at the look on my face when he asked that question.

"Do you have many people dying here, then?"

"Not yet." Said Norman, his face deadpan.

"No, I don't have any faith."

Again a long pause as he looked thoughtful.

"Would I respect others who did? "He asked firmly.

"Yes I would as long as I wasn't pestered."

A long silence followed the questions as Norman pondered my form. I had no idea which way the decision was going to go but I found myself really wanting to be here in the building, as if it was planned for me to be here. It was the strangest feeling but it felt as if I belonged here.

"As it happens we do have a spare room. When would you want it, Gary?"

"Now." I said very quickly just in case he changed his mind.

And so I found myself a resident in room 96 of the YMCA Norwich.

Snatched from the fire.

CHAPTER SIXTEEN

As I stepped into my new room I couldn't help but reflect on my diverse and varied accommodations of the past few months.

From lonely existence in a caravan at the bottom of Irish Georges garden, to Legion bunk beds, a stint sleeping rough and cold, then of course, the horror hostel; then my freezing cold Cortina and finally room 96 of the YMCA Norwich. What a journey it had been and just the thought of being alone and safe was a wonderful event for me. I didn't have to sleep with one eye open for trouble anymore.

The room wasn't big, no larger than a modern prison cell but it had a single bed, with sheets and pillows provided. There was a table and chair, some shelves and in one corner the oldest wardrobe I had even seen. It probably came off the Ark with Noah. A single large window looked out at a brick building across a sheltered courtyard below. Not much of a view but it was fine for me. It may have been small but to me it was better than a room at the Waldorf hotel.

As I looked around I caught sight of a book laid on top of the pillows and picked it up. It was a brown hard backed Gideon's bible. I couldn't remember a time in my life when I had picked one up and it felt kind of comfortable in my hands, as though it was meant to be there. Little did I know.

Norman had been standing in the doorway after showing me up to the room. He handed me the key, my key, and then wandered off. We had agreed to meet next morning to begin the process of signing on and filling in the forms that would enable the YMCA to claims the cost of my stay with them. As he left he said something that will be with me always, branded in my brain forever.

"You're safe here, Gary, and brought here at this time for a reason." Little did I know what that reason was.

The care system in the 'Y' was very good indeed and covered all aspects of life; body, mind and spirit and was represented by the YMCA's symbol, the red and black upside down triangle.

A full breakfast was provided as part of the cost of staying there and could be had in the canteen down by the reception, from 7.30 through to 9 am seven days a week. Meals and snacks could be bought at any time during the day and evening meals were ready from 5pm onwards. All food was subsidized and affordable and freshly cooked.

The doors were locked at midnight and opened at 6.30am because of the number of vulnerable residents living in under social service care.

The 'Y' was a safe and secure place to be although it did have its fair share of problems. But there was a good dedicated staff to help those who needed help. And there was no excuse for not being helped.

I sat down on the edge of the bed, abruptly feeling really tired and sleepy, like finishing a long distance walk. All I had with me was the clothes I was in; everything else was back in the boot of my car. I was so fatigued that I had trouble remembering where I had parked it.

With a huge exertion I stood and left room 96, locking it behind me and headed off to Baltic house to get that cash payment, then collect my gear from the car. I decided to leave the car where it was as there was nowhere to park here at the 'Y'. If I got a parking ticket, well, tough.

As I headed down the long staircase leading to the front exit doors I felt better than at any time I could remember for a long, long time.

I felt as if I were on the threshold of a better life.

My new routine began to 7am the very next day, after one of the best night's sleep I'd had for as long as I could remember. I wandered down to the canteen for my breakfast, one of many I was to enjoy during my time at the 'Y'. I know from my Army days that breakfast is one of the most vital meals of the day.

In the canteen you help yourself to cereals and tea or coffee, made your own toast in a rather ancient machine. Then you queued at the main hot plates, handed in your blue ticket, then had a full on English breakfast of fried eggs, bacon, sausages, beans, tomatoes, fried bread, all masterfully plonked right on your plate by the cook. Kippers could also be ordered as well as black pudding for the more adventurous or mad.

I sat down at a table well away from others and as I shoveled the food down I had my first real look at the other lads, my fellow inmates at the 'Y'.

Most were 18-22 years, with one or two older men there as well, looking as though they had been through the mill, then gone back for a second helping of trouble in life.

The younger lads had that been-through-the-care-system look about them, that institutionalized, prison-like posture of constantly looking around them like nervous birds when a cat was about. Most had pale faces as if they were afraid to venture outside the confines of the 'Y' and into the sun. On the whole they also had roll up cigarettes tucked behind their ears, like a badge of some club and had the customary spotty faces to match.

As the canteen filled up two lads came over and settled at the table next to me, both loud for the time of day, and obviously full of their own importance. I had seen them push in the line at the serving plates, the other lads deferring to them. Obviously they had a reputation of some kind.

One of them turned to me, pointed to the salt shaker on my table and said, "Salt." It was a command not a nice request.

He was a hard looking person, but not very bright. I simply said, "Get it yourself." and gave him my hard stare, which had an effect on him and he was suddenly visibly unsure of himself. I decided to carry on as I intended so I picked up the saltshaker and moved it further away from them.

I then switched my knife from left hand to my right, the action very clear. "Now try and get it." It was an outright challenge from me to them both. Others lads around us had cottoned on to the fact that a breakfast drama was unfolding rapidly. The canteen had gone reasonably quite.

The lad hesitated, no nerve at such an early hour, but the event hadn't gone unnoticed by the other lads. I turned back to my food, acting cool and unconcerned, totally ignoring the two. I even added some more salt to my food, adding insult to potential injury, looking at them both as I did so, just daring them to make a move.

When I had finished eating I stood to take my plate to a trolley with all the other empty utensils. As I passed the two lads I said loud enough so that those seated about could hear," Try that again and there'll be trouble. Understand?" and I stood over them until they both nodded, a bit awed by me standing over them.

There was a new guy on the block and they had better get used to it.

I left the canteen, heading for a nice shower feeling more than content with my first breakfast.

The next few days were spent getting into the system and I had all the help I needed, from form filling to telephone calls on my behalf to Chantry House, another DHSS building that dealt with housing benefits. Everyone was very helpful and for the first time in a long time I felt safe and supported.

Very soon I would also be getting a regular amount of cash while I looked for work that would enable me to live well in the 'Y' with evening meals and snacks, as I wanted them.

It honestly felt as though I was on holiday as I could sleep in or go back to bed after breakfast if I chose too. I could take a walk or stay in and read or watch TV or even have a game of snooker.

Life was definitely on the up and already the horrors of my time in France were starting to fade, like a bad bruise changing color until it was gone.

But then I met the strangest collection of people ever to cross my path and they were going to affect me for the rest of my life. Who were they?

The Christians.

And what a strange bunch they were!

The Young Men's Christian Association was founded in 1844 by a rather remarkable 23 year old man, one George Williams, who was a bit of a character, to say the very least.

He was the youngest of 8 children who became a Christian after a few years of being a 'careless, thoughtless, Godless, swearing young fellow', to use his own words. In London in the 1800's there wasn't a great deal to do in the evenings apart from drinking and chasing females, so he began to meet with a few others and this turned into the YMCA. The first members met in St. Paul's churchyard in 1844 in the heart of London. Since then it has become a worldwide organization without equal. In fact the year 2005 saw its 150th birthday. The urgent need to help young men and woman is as real today as it was in George Williams's day.

Norwich 'Y' was founded in 1856 and was based on solid Christian ideals and the Word of God, which the present day staff tries hard to keep up with.

Many of the staff there had a vibrant faith in God and did their level best to live their lives as worthy of the One who saved them, not easy in a hostile, at times, environment.

I avoided any kind of contact with the Christians and the regular meetings that were announced over the public address system. Bible studies and prayer meetings seemed to be going on at all times of the night and day and were open to all.

There was even a Pastoral advisor, a tough Scot called David McFarland, who had the look of one who'd been on the other side of the fence at some stage. He was a good guy but I kept well away just in case he attacked me with his bible. That was something for which I had no training to deal with.

Several of the lads had become Christians and had that new found fervor which made them very loud and the butt of many jokes and lots of ribbing. If this was what got them through the day, then fine for them. Everyone needed a little help to get by in this sad, untidy life.

But not for me. I managed alone.

To be perfectly honest I was more than surprised at the way the Christians acted, both those living in, the staff and those who came in from outside for the prayer meetings and so on. There was something different about these people. They seemed happy and enjoyed what they did. But there were a few things that turned me right off and caused me to question everything about them.

I couldn't believe it when the men started hugging each other in public with alarming regularity. It was all very gay and un- natural to me. Men hugging? No way! I resolved that if anyone of them tried to come anywhere near me then I would use extreme violence on them and blow the consequences. There would be some high drama.

There were limits in life and close contact between men was a line not to be crossed by me. No way, no how!

The second thing that struck me was that the Christians didn't use foul language in an environment where the F word was as common as sea salt. This made them stick out like roses in a pigsty. A light in the darkness. It may not seem like a big thing but in here it was and it got my attention.

So as the days passed I kept myself to myself enjoying own company and didn't show any interest in the God of these Christians.

But the God of the Christians was interested in me, as I was about to find out in the rather unlikely form of two of the greatest characters ever to cross my path.

Of all the people I met in those first days and weeks in the YMCA there were two men in particular who had quite an influence on my life at the time, and, to be honest, for the years that followed. Others had an effect but not in the same way as these two did.

One such person was John Drake, the General Secretary of the Norwich YMCA, who still held the post for nearly 30 years after we first met near the snooker table one morning.

I had no idea who he was but since his office was on the first floor above the canteen he was frequently seen moving about the building, like a man on a mission full of purpose.

John was, and still is, a tall distinguished guy who sometimes wears a goatee beard, who on our first meeting reminded me of an old oil painting I had once seen of a gentleman highway robber on horseback, holding up a coach at pistol point, very charming but with a hint of steel in his eyes.

John had a voice and eyes that were genuine when he talked with me and I liked that from the start as he introduced himself and shook hands with me. He chatted with me for several minutes but was aware of everyone coming and going, near and far. It seemed as though he knew every one of the lads by name and, as is John's way, had a word for all of them, all positive and friendly. I had never seen this before in anyone I had ever met.

He was a totally approachable guy but you knew for a fact that he was the boss.

As he took off at his normal high speed, several guys I had got to know all said the same thing to me; he was a safe kind of guy, praise indeed from those, who like me, had a cynical streak a meter wide. He wasn't bad for a Christian was the chat on the floors. High praise.

The second person that was to touch my life I actually heard a long way off before I ever first set eyes on him, a loud foghorn laugh and a coarse cockney voice to match.

Chris Simmons was about five foot four inches tall, with shoulders that were nearly was tall as he was, honestly reminding me of Fred Flintstone, the cartoon character. (I didn't know it at the time but we were to be lifelong friends until his tragic death in 2004).

Chris was on the staff of the 'Y' and was an ex-Parachute Regiment soldier, with a background of gangsters and villainy back in London, which was the family business. He had also been an alcoholic and was in recovery when we first met.

And, more importantly, he was a Christian of 14 months when our paths first crossed and he didn't care who knew it. Not even me.

Although I eventually came to love and have a long fruitful friendship with Chris, at first he was the most annoying person I had ever met in my entire life as he had decided that I needed Jesus Christ in my life and made it his sole mission to tell me the good news of the Gospel of Jesus!

To help pass the time of day the 'Y' always arranged a number of activity for the residents, one being football in the large indoor sports center at the back of the building. Chess was also another firm favorite for those with a brain and some of the chess matches got as heated as any premiership football match and the occasional fight broke out as well which was a bonus to an otherwise tedious game. I never knew chess could be so dangerous.

Many of the lads got involved but rugby was my game and pouncing about with a football held no interest for me at all. I only cheated at chess as I couldn't play well so I gave that a miss as well.

I soon found, that with a big full English breakfast every morning with snacks through the day and a large evening meal now my money was coming in, that I was beginning to put on a little weight.

So when Chris put the word around that he was opening a weight training gym in the basement I took up the challenge and joined the club.

In the first week a good number of lads turned up and it great to be a part of something that had purpose and an end result. Chris worked us all very hard and by the end of that first week, many of the lads had taken up the 'Y's favorite sport - laziness, and packed it in as Chris set a punishing regime of training.

So on the Monday of the second week it was just Chris and I, entombed in the chalky basement of the 'Y', and surrounded by heavy weights and the smell of very bad feet and sweat.

As we pumped iron Chris had a habit of saying 'Praise the Lord' every time he completed a set of weights and there were even times when I did as well as a kind of reflex as I'd heard him say it so many times!

At every opportunity he'd try to inject something about God into the conversation which was really bugging me. But I soon came to realize that he wasn't being insensitive or fanatical but he was in fact, in his own words, *"still bloody surprised that God wanted to even know a guy like me!"*

And thrilled he was about his new faith and as the days passed I found he was like a small boy with his first new bike at Christmas, pleased as punch and wanting to tell everyone about it.

In all my life I had never met someone so sure of what he believed, and in fact, not that many since. Chris wasn't the most articulate of people but what he lacked for in speech he more than made up with sincerity and conviction and I soon found myself thawing to him as I discovered that there were surprisingly similar events that had taken place back in our pasts, how alike we were.

So one afternoon, deep underground, I did the very thing I promised myself I would never do- I asked Chris what this Jesus feller was all about.

And what an answer I got!

CHAPTER SEVENTEEN.

"God's got very little to do with organized religion." Chris said as we paused to take a drink. If he had been surprised by my question, he hid it well. I knew that he had been angling for ages to get me to talk. "It's all about a living relationship with God who is as real as we're sitting here."

"A relationship? With who? "I asked.

"Jesus." The way Chris said the name was so very different from how most people said and used the name. He spoke it not as a swear word or curse but as he would a loved friends name. His normally harsh cockney voice always softened slightly, and when he said that name, Jesus, a smile was always present as well.

"Jesus?" I was surprised and showed it.

"Yeah. Jesus. Nice name isn't it."

"Oh, right." I got under some weights, ready to get back to the training. We had been doing bench presses. As I grunted and pushed, that name, Jesus, kept bouncing around inside of my head like an out of control rubber ball, crashing off walls.

I sat up after I had completed my repetitions, sweat dripping off me. "What's Jesus got to do with anything?" I took a long sip of water. "I thought he was dead?"

Chris laughed, the sound very loud in the confines of the gym, "You should know that you can't keep a good man down!" he looked me straight in the eye, as hard as a blow. "Gary, He is alive and kicking, mate!"

There was a long pause, the silence suddenly very loud; then I began to laugh, embarrassed by what Chris had said. I tried to bluff my way out of the condition.

"He's alive?"

Chris nodded.

"Then what's his room number here then?" I joked and stood ready to leave, as for some reason I was feeling extremely uncomfortable as if Chris had shared some deeply personal habit with me. As I climbed the steep stairs out of the gym, Chris called up after me, "Jesus loves you, Gary, and you can't run from that!"

Back in my room after taking a long hot shower, those parting words kept ringing in my ears, "Jesus loves you, Gary".

Yeah, right, I thought as a sudden surge of bitterness exploded in me as unexpected as stepping on a landmine, blowing off a foot.

He loved me so much that I didn't have a Dad!

Loved me so much with all the hard times as I grew up.

Loved me so much that I'd failed at everything, alienated my family and so on and on. I listed all my life's woes.

A nasty fury welled up in me as now I had a target; someone to blame, for all of life's unfairness and the way things had turned out for me. Until now I had just blamed it all on bad luck and circumstances. A bad roll of the dice.

But now I knew better; it was Gods fault and I was angry!

For the next few days I avoided Chris and all contact with just about everybody, as the anger boiled in me, as barely contained as a nuclear reactor going out of control. The pressure was building until eventually it was going to explode, big time. I knew the signs and I was looking for trouble.

At breakfast, normally my favorite time of day, no one came near where I sat as I glared and swore at anyone foolish enough to come too close to my table. I was looking for a fight and there were no takers.

Most days I would go out for a nice long walk around Norwich to think about things but now I was just hoping that someone would bump into me so I could have an excuse to lash out. I hadn't experienced such violence of heart for a long, long time. It was if darker forces than I could see or understand were rushing me headlong down a steep and icy slope with nothing but rocks at the bottom.

Back in the 'Y' I even cursed and swore at the staff as they passed by, for no other reason than that I knew they were these Christians who loved this Jesus so much. Just the mention of the name of Jesus was now enough to send me into a fit of cursing and foul language. I could no longer control my actions and it felt as if I had been taken over, a human marionette, danced about by hatred of this Jesus and His followers.

Even my dreams had taken on a sinister twist as murder and death and mutilation filled my mind almost as soon as I lay down to sleep. Trouble was, I was starting to enjoy the dreams.

One of the weekday prayer groups met in a room on my landing and as I passed by one afternoon I kicked and hammered on the door, shouting and swearing at those inside. Wisely they kept the door shut and prayed all the harder, no doubt!

It all came to a head one evening.

Chris was on night duty and was doing his security walk about, checking the building was secure and that no one was playing loud music and so on.

At one point we both found ourselves near the snooker table in the main lounge area at the same time. There were a good many other lads around, sitting chatting, waiting their turn on the snooker table to play. Others were on the dartboard having an intense match. A typical night in the 'Y'.

Chris just grinned at me. "All right, Gary!" he was cheerful and didn't care who knew it. He was just being Chris. If he had been offended by events of the last weeks of me ignoring him he didn't let it show.

"Xxxxx off!" I swore at him as loud as I could, guaranteeing he would get the message and fast. Every eye in the place turned to us, like a scene in a Wild West film when the gunslinger walks into the bar, ready to confront the bad guys. The whole 'Y' had been aware something was brewing and word had got around that I was fed up with the God bashers. Blood was scented and no one wanted to miss out what happened.

"That's not very nice, Gary."

"Are you deaf?" I was suddenly very cold, a sign that I knew only too well. Violence was now dangerously near the surface and was quickly reaching a point where I wouldn't be able to control it.

"No. I hear you. What's the matter with you?"

"What's up?" I stepped in very close. Chris didn't flinch an inch. I prodded him in his chest." You're getting on my nerves, Jesus man!"

Chris grinned, completely unaffected by my menaces. "Well, as I told you, Jesus does love you, mate."

"You say that one more time, I'll Xxxxx well hit you!" I jabbed him again in the chest.

He shrugged. "I'll just turn the other cheek, just as Jesus had to do." His voice was very calm, looking me straight in the eyes. There wasn't a trace of fear there. "I've been hit by bigger and better men than you, Gary." He shrugged.

I wanted so badly to attack but something restrained me, deep inside, as again I heard those word, *'Jesus loves you'*.

I turned and walked off leaving behind a lot of surprised and stunned onlookers at the confrontation that had taken place. There was also a little disappointment that there hadn't been a fight.

As I stormed up to my room and another night wrestling with the demons in my head, I made dark plans to attack Chris during the night as he made his rounds of the building. He worked alone and no one would ever now what had happened, or at least prove what took place.

I wasn't used to someone standing up to me when I had a go and it seemed that the voices in my head were taunting me now, urging me to seek revenge. And revenge always tasted nice.

What I didn't know was that a prayer campaign had just been launched that very day.

And I was the target!

It must of have been those praying Christians but that night I slept right through until morning and never carried out the act of violence I had been urged to do by what I by now called the Voice, the driving force behind much of the evil things I had done. The Voice was also the author of the deep depressions I sank into and the reminder of the past hurts that constantly sat at the front of my thoughts.

The Voice had a name but one I didn't know at the time.

The Devil.

A few days later, when I was calm enough, I went back down into the gym in the basement. Chris was already there and welcomed me back as if nothing had happened.

"Bit calmer now, mate?" was his only reference to things.

"A bit." I said and began to warm up ready to lift some serious weights. A part of me wanted to say sorry to Chris but I didn't know how too. So I decided to make amends by being polite to him and maybe even listen to him.

I enjoyed the training that day and I liked Chris being there. I had secretly begun to admire him for his faith. After all, he had stood up to me, even getting the Jesus bit in as well. He had guts and faith, a winning combination. He seemed to be living what he talked about.

As the days moved along we started to become firm friends and he told me, bit by bit, how he'd become a Christian after hearing the gospel from an ex- policeman, called Danny. His life had been a real mess with drinking, fighting and villainy.

So when he heard the good news about Jesus love for him, something clicked inside at the chance to begin a new life, with his past forgiven and forgotten by God, through the death of His son, Jesus.

Whenever Chris spoke of his faith he would nearly always say," It still feels too good to be true!" a firm look of surprise on his face, "That Jesus would die for someone like me."

We began to talk about many, many subjects and I found that I was becoming more comfortable as Chris explained small, basic facts about God, the Bible and Jesus. I asked many questions and if Chris didn't know, he said so and didn't try to bluff it out and always promised to find out. He didn't waffle or make things up.

I had loads of questions, the same as most people do if they are honest.

Who was God?

Who made this world and the creatures and people?

Why is there suffering and pain?

Why do bad things happen to good people?

Does God have a white beard?

Why can't we all go to Heaven?

Several time late at night he would knock on the door and tell me the answer to a question asked days before.

Slowly but surely, the words sank down deep into the murky hidden parts of my life, soothing my troubled mind as they acted like penicillin fighting a terrible infection of the soul.

The closed, reinforced gates to my heart and emotions were being pried open, bit-by-bit, as the Jesus of the Bible became more real.

David McFarland, the pastoral worker, called me into his office next to reception, for a 'wee chat', as he put it. Dave was a good bloke and reminded me in appearance of a young Jasper Carrot, the comedian.

He closed the door and I wondered what I had done wrong, or rather what I had been caught out on.

"You settling in ok?"

"Fine." I decided to be cautious.

"Good. Do you fancy a change of scenery for a wee while?"

"Depends on where and when." I had a sudden nasty feeling that I was about to be asked to leave and go somewhere else.

"I'm taking a group of 8 men down south to another YMCA, a place called Fairthorn Manor. It'll be a working trip helping to restore and build an old sailing boat, clearing the grounds and so on. Yes or no?"

Dave was always straight to the point, never beating around the bush. I doubted he even knew a bush was there!

"Sure." I shrugged. What harm could a trip away from here do?

"Good man, we leave on Sunday".

Fairthorn Manor was a YMCA national activity center situated near the small Hampshire village of Curdridge, 8 miles away from the seaport of Southampton, and was set in the middle of 111 acres of well looked after grounds.

It was a place where all kinds of activities took place, from canoeing on its very own lake, to crossing the Solent by canoe to make it to the Isle of Wight on a proper expedition led by the trained staff.

Sailing was also taught by in house instructors using a fleet of small wayfarers, complete with safety vessel to accompany them on trips.

Archery was another favorite and for the fit and mad there was a top class assault course, complete with initiative test section full of impossible things to do, which most groups relished and tackled with gusto.

The manor boasted good accommodations both in the main house but also out in the grounds in old style wooden huts that looked pre-war. The cookhouse was purpose built to feed the many who passed through the Manors doors each week and pumped out three good meals a day.

We arrived late Sunday night and after a breakfast next morning that competed seriously with the ones back in Norwich, we were taken down to the boathouse, right on the water's edge of the River Hamble, and saw for the first time the object of our visit; an old rotted out wooden boat of the type used by old whaling ships to row out after their prey, the whales.

It was an on-going project, far from completion and I wondered what on earth our little group would hope to accomplish in just five days before we left Friday night to head back home. But I supposed every little helps.

The work was really very simple. We sandpapered, planned wood or rubbed down planks of wood until they were smooth. By lunchtime it was more than obvious that there were too many people working at one time as there was only so much that could be worked on at any one time, especially by un-skilled hands like ours.

So after a good and very filling lunch it was decided that the other lads would work around the grounds under the scrutiny of the head grounds man. I was left alone with Dave to work on the whaler.

I often wonder if it was planned that way to get me alone with him and I had a fairly good idea that Chris had been talking about our conversations. I didn't mind actually.

So as we worked we talked about anything and everything- except faith and God, the very subject I reckoned that Dave was itching to talk about. So I made it a point not to raise the subject or anything that could even closely resemble religion. I wasn't going to rise to the bait.

But as the days passed, he didn't show the slightest inclination to say anything about this Jesus, but for all that I just knew that he had to be impatient to say something. If Chris was anything to go by then all Christians could talk about this Jesus at the drop of a hat. As far as I knew anything about Christians, it was their job to Bible bash, wasn't it?

So I kept on working away, just waiting for Dave to crack under the strain.

I was enjoying the challenge and was determined that I wasn't going to make it easy for him.

But by Thursday afternoon, just after another good lunch, it was ME who was starting to crack!

Whilst waiting for some probe from Dave, I had been doing nothing but thinking about things as we worked in companionable silence for hours on end. I enjoyed it and found myself wishing that I could do this full time.

I had realized just how many questions I had but there was also this kind of unnamed fear that I would be laughed at if I openly asked for answers from Dave. In a way I wanted to put the same questions as I had done with Chris, just to see if these Christians agree with each other.

By now I had even more questions that I just had to have the answers too!

Does God sleep?

What's this Jesus up to now?

What does Jesus do all day in heaven?

Why can't I see God?

And perhaps the greatest question of them all and one that is in the heart of every person alive on the planet today.

DOES HE LOVE ME?

I worked away until the questions built up a pressure of their own, like the fizz in a shaken bottle of champagne, straining to push the cork out with a loud POP!

Dave was being so annoyingly silent, as if he was waiting for me to make the first move.

Eventually I could bear it no longer and in a flash of anger, I turned to Dave, chisel in hand like a weapon and had a go at him, the words tumbling out like small children at playtime.

" This great and loving God of yours, " I began but Dave didn't flinch or even stop the work he was dong, sanding down a plank of wood, " If He's so great and loving and kind why do old ladies get raped in their own beds and all these little kids die of hunger!" I stepped closer to him like a deranged knife fighter.

"You tell me that and I'll believe in your God!" I was shouting by this time and couldn't help it, losing control of my emotions that seemed to have hijacked by some other force.

Dave stopped what he was doing, put down his wood and looked straight at me." Gary, if you're going to blame God for those things, then you'll have to believe He's real."

I didn't know what to say to this but Dave pushed on, pressing home the opening I had given him, like a boxer with a series of hard jabs to the body.

"And if you believe God is real, then you'll also have to accept the existence of the opposite of all that God stands for, and that's where the devil comes in." Dave stepped forward and patted my arm, not taking any notice of the chisel I held towards him, aggressively by any standard.

"He's the one who does all those terrible things, Gary, not God." He paused then hit me very hard with his next few words. "Jesus loves you, Gary and He always has and always will do. He's also got a good plan for your life."

It was all too much for me and I turned and walked quickly off, his words ringing in my ears as loud and as real as if being replayed through IPod earphones. I didn't know where I was heading to, just walking and following a pathway alongside the River Hamble, the smell of the stagnant water strong.

God loves me?

God has a plan for my life?

I started to repeat those words out loud, like memorizing unfamiliar directions, unwilling to forget the words and get lost.

As I stumbled along the pathway, the tears came, hot and stinging, roaring up from deep and secret places where hurt and pain and disappointment had made their dwelling for year after year, a lifetimes worth, unable to be brought to the surface and face the light of day and truth; padlocked and chained like some dangerous prisoners, locked away for mankind's good and safety.

So many memories of incidents and hurts I had never spoken of to anyone on the planet, and never will, raced out of the dark places and into the open, an unstoppable torrent of unbelievable hurt, so painful that I really thought that I was going to die there and then on the riverbank, all alone.

How could God love me?

Look at what I had done, how I had acted terribly to so many people.

It seemed as all my sins were stacked up very high next to me and I was seeing them for the very first time, understanding what I had done, face to face with my crime.

It took a while for me to calm down, like a frightened child slowly realizing what he feared was in fact a shadow on a wall. I just sat there on the riverbank, alone and unsure what exactly was taking place in and around me.

The words that Dave had spoken, the truths he had uttered, had shaken me to the very core of my being.

He was right; if I were going to blame God for the evil things that happened to people, then I would also have to accept that there was a person called the devil, who did the terrible things that caused so much pain in the world.

But how could I know God was truly there? How could I see with my own eyes this God I so badly needed to believe in?

As I sat there I began to look around at my surroundings, at the trees and the water flowing by just inches away. Ducks paddled by me with a knowing look as though they already knew the answer I was so desperately seeking after.

Who made us? And what about the animals? Surely it wasn't all down to the evolution process I had been taught at school? If that was the case then there couldn't be a God and everything was just down to sheer luck or misfortune, the whole of life hinging on the flip of a coin. And suddenly that seemed intolerable. But how could I be sure that God made us in His image?

As if to answer my question a beautiful white swan, the king of the birds, came swooping in the end of the stretch of river where I sat, flying in very low and fast, yet still gracefully, 2 or 3 feet above the water. He was headed right for me and would pass by in a few seconds right in front of me. I had a grandstand seat in a royal fly-past.

Suddenly everything else was forgotten as I simply sat and watched as the swan began its landing checklist; long neck swept back, wings outstretched, feet with big webbed landing gear pushed down, then touching the water like some great big flying boat, just feet away from me. Water splashed up as the swan slowed then became a majestic white vessel cruising the river. A powerful joy flashed through me at such a close encounter with such a beautiful creature. I whooped like the small innocent child that I had been a long time ago, laughing with happiness at the moment only I had seen.

Then a question popped into my head as real and as loud as a penny being dropped into a metal moneybox.

Who made that swan?

And just as quick as the question came to the answer right back to me, as loud and true as if the words had been spoken aloud by a human voice.

"I made the swan!"

I jumped up to my feet, whirling round to see who had spoken these words to me but found that I was alone on the riverbank. I checked for several yards up and down to see if anyone had followed me and had heard me talking to myself and then had spoken to me, playing some kind of a joke. But there was no one else anywhere near me.

I was alone.

And then I realized who had spoken to me.

It had been the voice of God!

A sudden thrill unlike I had ever known before or since crashed through me like electricity as a revelation of what had just happened registered in my slow moving brain.

God made the swan!

God made me!

God LOVES me!

I began to cry with the sheer joy of the knowledge.

By the time I got back to the boat yard it was nearly dinnertime. Dave was still there working away, apparently unconcerned as to where I had been all these hours.

The walk back to the boatyard was an incredible time for me as a fledgling belief in God was formed, as answers to the many questions now fitted into place, like pieces in a jigsaw that had baffled me.

A kind of peace had filled me, calming me, a happiness running through my veins that I had only ever felt when I was sitting on my Granddads lap, knowing I was safe and secure.

I kept saying 'God Loves Me!' as I walked along, sometimes even hopping like a child, skipping along.

As soon as I caught sight of Dave I shouted over to him, very loudly "Hey Dave! Guess what?"

Dave set down his tools and faced me, already grinning as if he knew what had taken place along the riverbank.

I stated simply. "I believe in God!" a massive grin covering my face. Dave smiled, held and his hand which I took and shook.

"Great news. That's the beginning, Gary."

I was slightly taken aback; what did he mean by beginning? I must have looked blank.

Dave carried on, his voice soft." Believing in God is the easy bit, in many ways. The next step for you is to accept and believe in His son, Jesus Christ. He is the savior of the world." Dave paused to let these words sink in." You're nearly there, Gary, just a few more steps." He nodded in approval.

It was back to this Jesus that Chris was always banging on about. It seemed that I just couldn't escape Him.

"Can't I just have and believe in God?"

"You could, but then you wouldn't have the salvation from your sins that Jesus died on the cross for. Ask when you're ready." Dave checked his watch." Time for dinner, come on!"

Two days later were left the wonderful ground of Fairthorn Manor and drove back to Norwich and the 'Y'.

My belief in the God of the bible had calmed me down, soothing every area of my life. Dave mentioned the fact that I hadn't sworn and used foul language since that afternoon, a fact I hadn't noticed at all. There was freshness about my thinking and I hadn't had the slightest desire for a drink.

But the next step was this Jesus feller.

God Himself seemed ok, as He was very big and somewhat aloof from day to day affairs, after all He had to take care of billions of people and kept the universe ticking over, a very hard job I imagined.

But Jesus?

It appeared as if things were about to get up close and personal with Him. I remembered what both Chris and Dave had said about Jesus leaving the splendor of heaven to become one of us for a time. If that was true than it was really something, to mix it up with the ordinary people of the world.

As I sat at the back of the battered minibus rattling its way back to Norwich, I had to admit that the thought of this Jesus was beginning to scare me.

If He was for real, then it seemed that there was no way of avoiding Him.

CHAPTER EIGHTEEN.

On my return to Norwich that evening, I found Chris and told him all what had happened; of the swan on the river and of God Himself speaking to me personally. I was almost breathless with excitement as I recounted in detail what I felt like now, of the changes taking place almost as fast as I could explain myself.

Chris was tickled pink and urged me straight away to take the next step and ask Jesus into my life as Lord and Savior. He was as keen as mustard.

"Come on, Gary, you know it makes sense." He said it a dozen times in as many minutes. He seemed even more excited than I was at what was taking place.

What he said did make sense and so, the very next day, I asked Chris to explain to me exactly what it was all about with this Jesus feller.

Starting at the very beginning I heard how man had been made by God, in His image and was a masterpiece of creation, designed to take care of the newly made planet earth. Also in the deal was a real life, real time relationship with God to walk and talk and have fellowship with Him in the Garden of Eden.

I was shocked to hear how easily man disobeyed what God had said, and by doing so, fell right into the devils evil schemes to get them to doubt the very words of God. One of Gods greatest gifts to us was freewill to make decisions. Sin now entered the world and the once open and very close relationship God had with Adam and Eve was now blocked. That's why we have death and disease and murder to this very day as man choose to turn away from Gods protective cover. That was one very big question answered for me.

But God wasn't caught short by any means and in fact He had never left Plan A, now putting into action a unique way to get man back to Him- by sending His own dear son, Jesus, as a sacrifice for man's sin. Someone had to pay the terrible price and it fell to the innocent Jesus.

As Chris talked and shared the gospel, or good news, with me, I felt like a thirsty man discovering water in a very dry and dangerous place, as if life itself was in the water.

I heard how Jesus was born in way no man ever had before or since; born of a Virgin, a young girl called Mary. It's a common fact that the blood a child receives is of his father's blood group; that meant that Jesus had divine blood running through His veins and was therefore sinless and perfect and able to be the sacrifice because He was pure. He was both God and Man. Somehow I understood not with my head, but deep in my heart.

I listened in awe as I heard of the things Jesus did, of His love even for dirty filthy lepers. He touched and loved beggars and talked to them, which struck a chord with me, and made them whole and well. I heard how he did His best to speak to all he came across. When I found out that He had even raised the dead back to life, including one little girl, I was stunned.

I was so impressed that Jesus would leave the mind blowing splendor of heaven and come down to us, God with us, to show us that we hadn't been forgotten by a distant God.

He was here, mixing it up with the prostitutes and the druggies and the homeless. He treated rich and poor alike, showing no distinction between men and He definitely loved the un-lovely. I had a sudden flash back to the hostel back in France. I just knew he would've befriended every one of those human wrecks there, not alarmed when someone was sick into their soup.

I sat and cried when Chris told me of the hatred that finally led, after three years, to Him being beaten by Roman soldiers and ripped to bits when cruelly whipped and then, betrayed by all his friends, was hammered to a Roman wooden cross and left to die, with two villains next to him.

I was horrified to hear that people came and spat at him and taunted Him as he hung there, in agony. The God who suffered for those He loved.

I was transfixed to hear that ALL the sin of the world, from the beginning to the end and of every person who had ever lived or ever would, was placed on Jesus as He hung on the cross.

Jesus was innocent, yet made guilty, and therefore had to pay the terrible price of sin, and that was death. Yet Jesus willingly went to the cross because, in His massive love for us, He knew that this was the only way that the barrier between God and Man could be torn down.

And such was the awfulness of the price Jesus had to pay that He felt separated himself and cried out on the cross," My God, My God, why have you forsaken me?"

And then Jesus died, really died and not fainted; a Roman soldier delivered the coup de grace and stuck a spear in His side to make sure he was dead and blood and water came out. Definitely dead and not pretending.

As Chris talked it got very difficult to stay seated as it was like hearing a blow-by-blow account of the death of a loved one, someone very close and their final moments. I'd never known such emotion as that moment.

I heard for the first time of a man called Joseph of Arimathaea, who gave a tomb for Jesus, who was secretly a disciple. I was told of disciples who failed terribly just when it mattered and of the disbelief felt by those close to Jesus when He was placed in the tomb at His words that he would indeed rise after three days.

But the story was only just beginning as early Sunday morning, just as Jesus said, there was a huge surprise in store for everyone.

The two Mary's went to the tomb, hoping for a chance to anoint the body of Jesus- but when they got there the stone to the entrance had been rolled away and the grave clothes laying there, empty and folded; and there was an Angel sitting there and said, *"Why do you look for the living among the dead? He has risen!"*

Chris cried himself as he explained to this poor sinner how death was now gone, Hell defeated, and salvation and forgiveness of sin open to anyone who called upon the name of Jesus and asked for forgiveness.

Jesus was alive and appeared too many people as proof of His resurrection from the grave. He even had breakfast with some disciples on the seashore.

I remember my emotions as never before as the revelation of who Jesus was and what He had done suddenly became too much for me and I had to leave Chris alone. I needed space to take it all in as I was in no doubt that Jesus was real and alive and really did want me to know Him in a real and personal way.

I went for walk, my mind spinning.

When I returned back to room 96 later that day I was in turmoil of mind and soul like never before.

I knew that all Chris and Dave and John Drake and Ron Day (another good guy who had talked with me), had said was true down to the very last detail. But the Truth is difficult to handle if you're a stranger to its use.

I paced around the confines of the room, my thoughts jumbled like an out of control circus act, everything so confused- yet so very clear. I remember once as a boy climbing to the highest diving board at the outdoor swimming pool in Beccles in a fit of bravery, trying to impress Granny. I had stood right on the very edge of the concrete rim, toes hanging off the edge before I realized just how high I was above the water. Fear almost paralyzed me that day and I felt right now the same terror that had threatened to turn me to stone that day. I jumped that day and conquered the fear.

Fear of the unknown is a scary sensation.

I knew that I needed this Jesus in my life; the how of it I would get to later.

But there was still something that hadn't quite fallen into place and I couldn't put my finger on it. Strangely enough I felt the same way as I had on the riverbank as though something was about to happen, a Divine breathing space in events. What was it?

In the corner of the room, on the shelf, was a brown book I'd never once picked up. It was the Gideon's bible. If I didn't have a use for something then I don't touch it until needed. I was drawn like a moth to a flame to the bible and picked it up.

I sat down on the bed and opened it up, deciding to read the first thing that I found. Who knows, maybe God would speak to me through its pages. It was His book after all!

Taking a deep breath before the plunge into the unknown, I opened up the bible and looked down at what was written on the pages.

'Come to me, all you who are weary and burdened
And I will give you rest. Take my yoke upon you
And learn from me, for I am gentle and humble in
Heart and you will find rest for your souls. For my
Yoke is easy and my burden is light.'
Mathew chapter 11v28-30.

In that moment as I read the very words of Jesus, I knew that I knew that I knew that I needed this very Jesus more than anything in this world.

I was weary of life, I needed rest for my soul and here, in His book the bible, He promised to do exactly that. I was both stunned and amazed at how the words fitted exactly to my life at this exact moment in time. It just HAD to be God!

I decided in that instant to pray but wasn't sure how to do it.

Did I stand, sit or kneel?

Did I keep my eyes open or shut tight?

Did I have to be smartly dressed with a tie on or would jeans and the t-shirt I wore be all right?

Did I call God 'Sir' when I spoke to Him?

I had no idea but went ahead anyway. I figured that if He sat down to eat with lepers and prostitutes that I would be all right as I was.

I looked up at the ceiling, felling very uncertain.

'Dear Jesus. I've mucked up my life. You know that. If you're there then I want you to come into my life and change me because I've mucked it all up. Thanks for taking the time to listen.' I paused the quickly added a fast 'Amen' to end my prayer.

In that instant I was aware of a huge wave of sheer love and acceptance crashing into the room and I knew in that moment that it was all true. Jesus was alive and was responding to my call for help. Once and for all time I now knew He was there and was after me and did in fact love me!

WOW!

Two things happened in the seconds after that prayer.

One. I believed in this Jesus.

The second was that I was so terrified by what had just happened that I ran out of the room as the experience was so real that I thought that Jesus Himself had turned up!

Ten minutes later I found Chris and told him what had happened in the room. He was stunned, then elated as I told him in no uncertain terms that I wanted to give my life over to become a follower of Jesus Christ and could we do the business as soon as possible!

Then the funniest things of all as I told Chris that I thought that Jesus was in the room, so real was the experience a few minutes before.

So we hurried down the corridor to my room and we both carefully looked around the door frame, checking to see if Jesus was in the room!

I can laugh about this now but that day it was so real and vivid that I even checked inside the wardrobes! I didn't yet know about the Holy Spirit.

So, back in room 96, Chris explained the sinner's prayer to me, which was a confession of my sin, not to Chris, but to God through Jesus, a plea for forgiveness and a firm promise to follow Jesus for the rest of my life. It was as simple as A-B-C.

Chris then made sure that I knew exactly what was happening and so we came to most important moment of my life, the prayer of acceptance. It went something like this.

'Dear Lord Jesus. I come to you as a sinner needing your forgiveness, admitting that I have sinned. I ask you take my sin away through the blood spilt on the cross. I turn away from my past and promise to follow and serve you all the days of my life.

I believe you rose from the dead and are alive today and one day coming back for me.

Amen.'

And with that, I, Gary Wayne Ernest Moore, entered the Kingdom of Heaven and was wonderfully and gloriously born again, just as Jesus said. (If you have been touched by what you have just read then say the prayer as well!).

I sat there for a few precious seconds just savoring the moment, a delicious peace and calmness filling me from head to foot, eyes closed, and I knew without a shadow of a doubt that my life had just changed forever.

I opened my eyes and the first thing I saw was Chris walking across the room towards me with his arms wide open, ready to give me a hug!

"Oh NO!" I said aloud as he grabbed me, his newborn brother in Christ, and gave me a huge bear hug, and kissed me on the cheek!

But you know what?

It was a great welcome into a new life!

CHAPTER NINETEEN.

The change in my life was both immediate and, in some ways, dramatic. I stopped drinking almost straight away for one thing.

As the first few days after my conversion to Jesus Christ moved along I saw for myself first hand evidence of my new life, of the fact that I had been born again of the spirit of God and was in fact, what the bible called a new creation.

One day I had my usual walk and was passing through the crowded market place when a man barged into me, nearly knocking me over. Just a few short days ago I would've attacked him; instead, today, I asked him if he was all right! He was the most surprised man in Norwich that day, the more so when I began to talk to him about my Jesus. He was amazed, shaking his head as he left me. A small crowd had gathered and I told them as well about my Jesus!

I began to smile at everybody I met; the joy of knowing Jesus loved me just overflowing from deep inside of me, from heart to face muscles.

30 years later and I'm still smiling.

The second extraordinary event that took place in those first days challenged me to the very core as it involved violence.

One afternoon there was an argument between two residents. One of the staff members, a lovely guy called Ron Day (I was best man at his wedding years later) tried to calm down the incident as it was right on the point of turning nasty.

I was in the snooker area when it started and so I went over to back Ron up in case he needed any help. He was a Christian brother and that was good enough for me.

Ron was in-between the two guys and I could see one of them was about to have a go so I pulled Ron aside and stepped in the middle- just as one of the guys threw a punch at the other. Fortunately it hit me instead of Ron and there followed a stunned silence as the gathered crowd waited to see what happened next. I still had a reputation as a nasty piece of work and had only the week before thrown someone down the stairs for getting in my way.

I had been a Christian for four days now but I had read in the bible only that morning about turning the other cheek when violence was offered to you.

So I did; and then invited both the guys for a coffee in the canteen and told them all about my Jesus. Within a week both of them had also received Jesus as Lord!

It wasn't until later that night that realized what a test I had been through. It would've been so easy to have had a go back at the two lads. It seemed that Jesus was working on areas that I never thought possible to change.

And this was just the beginning of it all.

I wondered what was going to happen next.

Let me ask you a couple of questions.

Can God take a life, once useless and hopeless, and turn it around for His Glory?

Yes, He can.

Can Jesus do what He says He can in His word, the Bible?

Yes, He can.

Well, you may ask, how do you know for sure?

Simply put, because I'm one whose has been 'snatched from the fire.'

THE END.

(Or is it?)

✠

Finale

In the introduction to this simple book I told you about the car crash that so very nearly ended my life.

In the aftermath that followed that terrible day I spent four weeks battling just to stay alive in Maidstone hospital, Kent, under the amazing care of the ITU team there. My list of injuries was pretty impressive with left chest flail which left me unable to breath unaided because of the internal damage done when the ribs ripped into my lungs and this injury was right there at the top of the list of nasty's. My left arm was very badly smashed with several nerves severed irreparably and even today I don't have full use of this hand and arm.

And of course there was the almost total recall of the fire and nearly burning alive that kept replaying in my mind with vivid color and sound, complete with the smell of burning and a sense of the heat of those awful flames.

These flashbacks was for me perhaps the most harrowing part of what happened as the horror kept gripping me as real as if it was happening there and then.

Many miracles took place those first weeks and one of my favorites is the day that my wife, Jane, prayed for my kidneys to start working as they had packed up and were pushing me into cardiac arrest. A nasty situation to be in. I was on something called hemodialysis which cleans the blood through a machine then passes it back into the body, but what was happening was that my blood was clotting as fast as it was leaving me and couldn't be returned to my body. A crisis indeed. Thank God for blood donors as I used up plenty those days.

My Jane laid hands on me and prayed a very simple heart felt prayer." Kidneys work in the name of Jesus."

About twenty minutes later standing there with the amazing nurse Hannah, Jane was rejoicing over a bag of urine at my bedside which meant that the kidneys were working again. An impossible act in so many ways.

This was one of so many miracles as God began to heal me. It was the first but wouldn't be the last.

After I was stable enough to stand a chance of living I was transferred to King College hospital in London by ambulance due to a spinal fracture.

Again it was found that the fracture was 'healing itself' but again we believe this was the power of many Christians praying throughout the world.

For three weeks while in Kings College London, I was still ventilated using a tracheotomy in my throat and couldn't breathe alone or even speak. This was terrifying for me and there were several incidents which still cause me to shudder even to this day, some years later, when things didn't go as planned. Especially one very dark night when I nearly lost my life there as things went downhill with the speed of sound, the nurse on duty only just reacting in time as I stopped breathing, unable to do a single thing to help myself.

Through this time Jane travelled to London every other day not knowing what she would find and if ever there was a woman of faith, it was her. She may be small in stature but she's mighty in faith.

You see, the accident happened on 11th January 2011 and we were supposed to be getting married on the 16th April 2011. Poor timing on my part.

Several friends suggested postponing the wedding but we stood firm, clinging to the word that our God has spoken to us about the day and date, 16th April.

And that was good enough for us. God's word is there to be stood upon as a rock in times of trouble and fear and that's all we did.

When I was well enough to travel I was transferred to the William Harvey hospital in Ashford, Kent, much closer to Canterbury where we lived and attended City church.

Once there the hard work began as I couldn't walk due to muscle loss and the fact that I now only had the use of one hand, my right.

The left hand and arm were not much use and so I had to begin to relearn the basics of life, including how to walk again.

But I had my lovely Jane to help and love me back to health.

In hospital I was still experiencing terrible flashbacks to the crash and I knew that my mind had been damaged by what I had experienced. There wasn't an hour that went by it seemed when I didn't go through the trauma.

I have always understood the healing power of my Jesus but now it seemed that I needed a miracle beyond anything I could ever have of imagined. I needed my mind to heal from the post-traumatic stress that was making me sick.

I just knew that this was going to be the biggest battle of all.

As I lay there in that hospital bed I simply asked God to heal my mind as there was no way I wanted to take that trauma home with me. So I very simply asked my Jesus to heal my mind, reasoning that He made it so He could heal it!

I didn't have a blinding flash of light but I just felt different after that simply prayer.

A week later I was discharged and went home on a Friday night.

That Saturday I was alone with Jane and that's when God touched me with His healing as we sat and cried for several hours at all that had gone on and the horrors we had faced together.

All I had to do was to try and live, often unaware what was happening to me, but my Jane had to face each day over several months and battle through. She has her own story to tell of this time and her adventure into discovering the character of God.

And did we get married on the date we had been given?

Yes we did and what a glorious day it was as we not only celebrated our marriage but the amazing victory over adversity and a God that had snatched me from the fire.

Thank you for reading this humble offering and I hope that you too will find Jesus as well.

Gary Moore.

Let me have the last word.

By reading this book I will hope that you are in no doubt that I have a very real and vibrant faith and that's in the person of Jesus.

It's all so very easy to read something and then put the book down and say, "Oh that was nice".

However, just as life itself can be a huge challenge, I feel that I have to challenge you, the reader, about where you stand with my Jesus, the Jesus of the Bible, and the One who is intimately interested in you.

You see, Jesus loves you just as you are; but He loves you too much to leave you as you are.

The biggest gift that Jesus offers is eternal life in Him.

The second and wonderful free gift is the very real opportunity to make a brand new and fresh start in life and to live just as God intended you to be in the first place.

So, what is this good news about Jesus?

Well here is the Gospel of Jesus in a few short lines.

THE GOSPEL.
(Good News)
OF JESUS.
And what it means for you.

God made the earth.

God made Man.
Man sinned.
God still loved us.
God reached out to us.
God sent His very own Son, Jesus.
He came down to us.
He loved us.
He died for us.
He rose from the dead.
He's coming back for us again.
HE LOVES YOU.

Let me leave you with three reasons why you need Jesus.

ONE. YOU HAVE A PAST
TWO. YOU NEED A FRIEND
THREE.HE HOLDS YOUR FUTURE.

If you would like to begin a personal relationship with Jesus today, then please pray this very simple prayer.

Lord Jesus Christ,
I am sorry for the things I have done wrong in my life.
I ask your forgiveness,
Thank you for dying on the cross for me to set me free from my Sins.
Please come into my life and fill me with your Holy Spirit and be With me forever.
Thank you Lord Jesus. Amen.

If you have prayed this very simple prayer, then please contact me at;

Garymoore1961@hotmail.com

And second is that I want you to contact a good church near to where you live and get involved in the life of that church.

You need to grow and learn and not just **survive**, but to learn to **thrive** as that's Gods will for you.

Be blessed,
Your big brother in Jesus,
Gary.

Printed in Great Britain
by Amazon